THEATRUM SCOTIÆ.

CONTAINING THE

PROSPECTS

Of Their MAJESTIES

CASTLES and PALACES:

Together with those of the most considerable

TOWNS and COLLEGES;

The RUINS of many Ancient

Abbeys, Churches, Monasteries and *Convents,*

Within the said KINGDOM.

All Curiously Engraven on COPPER PLATES.

With a SHORT

DESCRIPTION

Of each PLACE.

By *JOHN SLEZER,* Captain of the Artillery Company, and Surveyor of Their MAJESTIES *Stores* and *Magazines* in the Kingdom of SCOTLAND.

LONDON,

Printed by *John Leake* for ABELL SWALLE, at the *Unicorn* at the West-End of St. *Paul's Church-Yard,* MDCXCIII.

Title page of the Theatrum Scotiae *(1693) from the handcoloured and gilded copy in the National Library of Scotland's Rosebery Collection.*

A Vision of Scotland

The Nation Observed by John Slezer 1671 to 1717

Keith Cavers

H M S O

NATIONAL LIBRARY OF SCOTLAND

British Library Cataloguing in Publication Data

A catalogue record for this book is available from the British Library

ACKNOWLEDGEMENTS

I am grateful to the following who have given me encouragement and assistance in the preparation of this book. Geoffrey McNab; Alethea Hayter; the estate of the late A.K. Slessor; Peter G. Vasey of the Scottish Record Office; Sheena McDougall of the Edinburgh Room, Edinburgh City Libraries; Ian Gow of the National Monuments Record of Scotland; and, at the National Library of Scotland, Margaret Wilkes, Alan Marchbank, and especially Kenneth Gibson for his invaluable help. I am also particularly indebted to John G. Dunbar for reading the manuscript and bringing a number of Slezer's drawings to my attention.

Editor: Kenneth Gibson (National Library of Scotland)
On-site photography: Keith Cavers
Slezer plate photography: Steve McAvoy (National Library of Scotland)
Picture research: Barbara Hegarty (National Library of Scotland)
Design: Derek Munn (HMSO Graphic Design)

ISBN 0 11 494245 5

0287546 C30 C/93 (C3808)

Contents

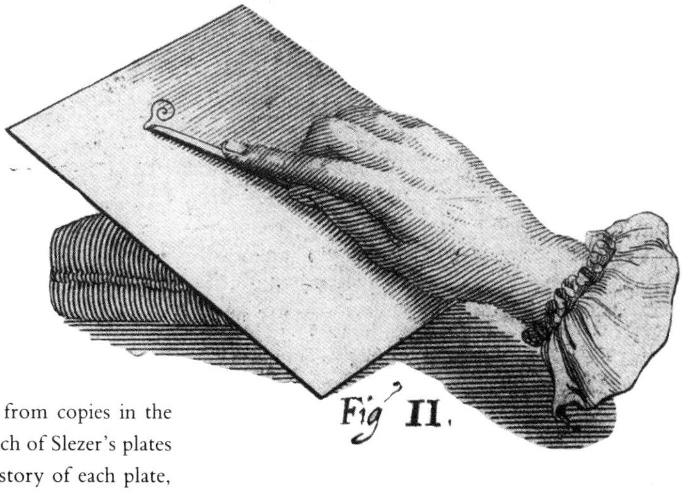

Fig **II**.

NOTE

Unless otherwise indicated, Slezer's plates and drawings are reproduced from copies in the collections of the National Library of Scotland. For ease of consultation, each of Slezer's plates has been given a number ('SL.1', 'SL.2' etc.); details of the publishing history of each plate, and of references to it in the present volume, are given under that number in Appendix II.

FORTROSE

ELGIN   GORDON

INVERNESS

ABERDEEN

DUNOTTAR

BRECHIN
MONTROSE
GLAMIS
ARBROATH
DUNKELD   DUNDEE
SCONE
PERTH   ST ANDREWS
FALKLAND
DUNBLANE   WEMYSS
ALLOA
STIRLING   DUNFERMLINE   BASS ROCK
CULROSS   HADDINGTON
DUMBARTON   EDINBURGH
LINLITHGOW   MUSSELBURGH
PAISLEY   GLASGOW   HATTON   DALKEITH
BOTHWELL   ROSLIN
HAMILTON   LAUDER
MELROSE
DRYBURGH   KELSO

AYR

CROSSRAGUEL

EST NOBILIS IRA LEONIS

SLEZER'S
SCOTLAND

INTRODUCTION

On 6 June 1693 Queen Mary signed a licence in favour of John Slezer, the Captain of her Artillery Train in Scotland, permitting him to publish the first of a series of volumes which would constitute a complete record of the Scottish nation.

Slezer was a remarkable man. A German adventurer who had made his home in Edinburgh in the 1670s, he had taken it upon himself to publish a detailed record of Scotland, and had spent the next twenty years of his life carefully depicting the principal sites of his adopted homeland.

By 1693, Slezer was ready to publish the first fruits of his labours, and, after being granted a licence by the Queen, proceeded to publish his celebrated *Theatrum Scotiae*. The book was a lavish volume consisting of fifty-seven engraved plates accompanied by written descriptions, and constitutes the first systematic illustrated record of Scotland, showing – as no other documents do – what the country actually looked like 300 years ago.

Today, many of Slezer's plates are well known through their frequent use in history books of all kinds. But Slezer himself, and the full extent of his various projects – including his plan to produce an even more ambitious publication called 'The Ancient and Present State of Scotland' – remain largely unknown.

The following chapters look in detail at Slezer's *Theatrum Scotiae* and how it was produced; they examine the plates and drawings destined for 'The Ancient and Present State of Scotland' but never published as intended; and they explore the fortunes of the man who was responsible for a body of work which gives a unique insight into Scotland's past.

MARIE R.

WILLIAM and MARY by the Grace of God, King and Queen of England, Scotland, France and Ireland, Defenders of the Faith, &c. To all our Loving Subjects, of what Degree, Condition and Quality soever, within Our Kingdoms and Dominions, Greeting. Whereas Our Trusty and Wellbeloved *John Slezer*, Gent. hath represented unto Us, That he hath been at considerable Charge, and great Pains in finishing the First Volume of a Book, Entituled *Theatrum Scotiæ*; and that he intends to Publish Two other Volumes upon the same Subject, and hath humbly besought Us, That in Consideration of the great Charge he will be at in perfecting the same, We would be pleased to Grant him Our Royal License for the sole Printing and Publishing the said Book, wherein We are pleased to Gratifie him; We do therefore hereby, Grant unto him the said *John Slezer*, Our Royal License for the sole Printing and Publishing the said Three Volumes of the said Book, Entituled *Theatrum Scotiæ*, or any of them, and do strictly Charge, Prohibit and Forbid all Our Subjects to Reprint within Our Kingdoms the said Books, or any of them, or any Abridgment, or any part of any of them, or to Import, Buy, Vend, Utter or Distribute any Copies or Exemplaries of the same, or any Part thereof Reprinted beyond the Seas, for the Term of Fourteen Years next Ensuing the Publishing hereof, without the Consent and Approbation of the said *John Slezer*, his Heirs, Executors or Assigns, as they and every of them so Offending will answer the contrary, not only by the Forfeiture of the said Books, Copies or Exemplaries, but at their utmost Peril, whereof as well the Wardens and Company of STATIONERS of Our City of *London*, as all and singular Our Officers of the Customs in this Port of *London*, or any other Place within Our Dominions, and all other Officers and Ministers whom it may concern, are to take particular Notice, That due Observance be given to this Our Royal Command.

Given at Our Court at White-Hall, the 6th. Day of June, 1693. *In the Fifth Year of Our Reign.*

By Her MAJESTY's Command.

J. TRENCHARD.

Royal licence of the Theatrum Scotiae *(1693)..*

John Slezer, Plan of Edinburgh Castle. British

The LIFE AND WORK OF JOHN SLEZER

Very little information survives about the early career of John Abraham Slezer, and most of what we do know comes from his own writings. He was probably born sometime before 1650 in part of German-speaking Europe, and was described as a 'high German' by his commanding officer, which may mean that he came from the upper Rhineland. Another indication of his Germanic origins lies in the spelling of his surname, which, as was common in the seventeenth century, could vary considerably. Variants like 'Slatcher', 'Sletzer', and 'Schletzer' are found – and, in an extreme case, 'Fletcher' – which suggests that the original pronunciation was the Germanic 'Schletzer'.

Slezer must also have been trained in military matters somewhere on the Continent, gaining practical experience in the fields of artillery and surveying, for when he subsequently moved to Scotland he was able immediately to take up a senior military post as Chief Engineer.

The Move to Scotland

Slezer first visited Scotland, he says, 'upon my travels in the year 1669',[1] and although he had the encouragement of several of the Scots nobility, he was not at that time able to gain immediate employment. He did, however, make strong contacts with men in positions of power, the Earls of Argyle and Kincardine in particular, and they were subsequently able to secure him the position of Chief Engineer for Scotland. His commission was issued on 23 December 1671 and he gave up his employment abroad and travelled back to Scotland to take up his new appointment.

As part of the duties of Surveyor of his Majesties Stores and Magazines (a post which Slezer held in parallel with his job as Chief Engineer), he was required to report on the state of fortifications in Scotland. At this time the main garrisoned strongholds were Edinburgh, Stirling, Dumbarton, Blackness, and the Bass Rock, the latter being gifted to the Duke of Lauderdale during this period. Slezer worked on the production of a set of groundplans of these castles, and it was during his travels at this time that he formulated a plan to repay the kindness and preferment that he had

John Slezer's marriage contract.
SRO RD14/Box40/792 published
with the permission of the Keeper
of the Records of Scotland.

enjoyed in Scotland[2] by producing a book of illustrations of the principal buildings, castles and towns of Scotland. In this he was encouraged both by Charles II and his brother the Duke of York (later James VII), who served as High Commissioner in Scotland and resided in Holyrood House from 1678 to 1683.

This type of project was not totally new. Volumes of views of buildings had been produced in France, and in England David Loggan was working on a record of the universities of Oxford (1675) and Cambridge (1688). Loggan had been a close associate of Wenceslaus Hollar, King's Scenographer or Designer of Prospects to Charles II, whose town views served as a model for Slezer. Other contemporary models include Dugdale's *Monasticon Anglicanum*, and Elias Ashmole's *The Institution, Laws & Ceremonies of the most Noble Order of the Garter* (1672), which both had illustrations by Hollar. What was new about Slezer's undertaking, however, was its comprehensiveness. This was the first time that anyone had set out to make a visual record of an entire nation.

Slezer was promoted Lieutenant to the Scots Train of Artillery in addition to his duties as Surveyor sometime around 1677, and in that same year he further consolidated his ties with Scotland by marrying Jean Straiton, the daughter of a military family, one of whose members was to become a Captain in the Jacobite army of 1715 and a prominent Jacobite agent. In time, Slezer had three sons: John (the eldest), who followed his father into the artillery, David, and Charles. There may have been more children, as Slezer mentions his 'numerous family' at a time when John at least was already in employment. (Later generations of the family were to alter the pronunciation and the spelling of the family name to 'Slessor', and the family have continued to play an active role in their adopted country's armed forces down to the present day.)

Slezer's integration into Scottish life continued when he was made a burgess of Dundee in 1678, of Linlithgow in 1682, and of Edinburgh in 1684. The following year he was made a free burgess of Edinburgh. A burgess ticket allowed the holder to trade within the burgh, but if Slezer was involved in some trade other than his military service at this time, no record has survived of it. It is known, however, that in 1681 he was sent to Holland to purchase guns and to recruit gunners for the Scots Artillery Train. During his six months travelling around Holland, he had great difficulty in finding any soldiers with sufficient artillery experience, as his letters testify.[3] Throughout his military career he tried to modernise the Scots (later the British) Artillery in Scotland, but his many recommendations and warnings were not heeded. The sorry state of the Artillery at the rising of 1715 proved Slezer's assessment to have been accurate.

The Making of the *Theatrum Scotiae*

As Chief Engineer, Slezer was in a good position to travel around the country taking prospects of towns and buildings. ('Prospect' was a contemporary term for a landscape view.) We are fortunate to have a contemporary record of Slezer soliciting support for his project. In 1678 his travels took him past Glamis, where Patrick, Earl of Strathmore was refurbishing the family castle which had fallen into some disrepair. The Earl recorded Slezer's visit in his 'Book of Record', a day book in which were recorded the activities of the household.

> *I have indeed been att the charge to imploy on[e] who is to make a book of the figure of the draughts and frontispiece in Talyduce★ of all the Kings Castles, Pallaces, towns, and other notable places in the Kingdome belonging to privat subjects who's desyre it was att first to me, and who himselfe passing by deemed this place worthie of the taking notice of. And to this man (Mr Sletcher by name) I gave liberall money because I was Loath that he should doe it att his owne charge and that I knew the cuts and ingraving would stand him mony.*[4]

This shows that by 1678 Slezer's scheme was well under way, and that, even at this early stage, he intended to make a feature of private houses as well as of the castles, palaces, and towns which one might expect to appear in such a work. It also shows that he was already soliciting for its finance, and understood the system of publication by subscription, where advance payments would significantly reduce the publishing risk. A year before this, he had also obtained private sponsorship from the most powerful man in Scotland at that time, John, Duke of Lauderdale: in return for his investment of £20, Slezer engraved plans of Lauderdale's home, Thirlstane Castle, along with two views of the Castle.

Today, the printing of images is taken for granted, but in the seventeenth century the reproduction of any image was a complex, laborious, and expensive business, involving large numbers of highly-trained workers who specialised in the production of the copper plates required to produce prints of a high quality. The reproduction of images by engraving a design in a metal plate, filling the engraved lines with ink, and squeezing the plate and a sheet of paper through a press, was first developed around the 1460s. Engraving proper uses a burin – a fine wedge-shaped chisel – to cut out a

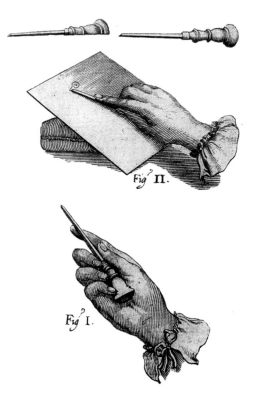

Engraving tools from Abraham Bosse, Traicté des manieres de graver en taille douce sur l'airin *(Paris, 1645).*

★ draughts = plans; frontispiece = front elevation; Talyduce = engraving, from the French 'taille douce'.

groove in the metal plate; but in the seventeenth century, and especially in Holland, the etching process began to take the place of engraving. This involves scratching through a waxy protective coating with a needle to create the lines which are then etched by a corrosive liquid. The etching process had been known for centuries, but in the seventeenth century materials became more readily available and etching was taken up as a medium by artists, especially the Dutch, with Rembrandt in particular making the most of its expressive capabilities.

The reproductive printmaker was a highly-skilled craftsman, not necessarily himself an accomplished artist, who was capable of translating an artist's drawing or design onto the copper plate for printing. For the printmaker, the benefit of etching was its speed of execution, and even where pure engraving was necessary in the finished plate etched lines could be used as a guide for the engraving tool. Very often, plates contain a mixture of both etching and engraving. The problem with etching, as opposed to engraving, is that the etched lines are neither as clean cut (being caused by chemical action) nor as deep as similar engraved lines, so etched lines tend to wear out more quickly.

When Slezer came to have the plates for his *Theatrum Scotiae* made, they were manufactured both in London and in Holland. The London plates are somewhat severe, and are composed mostly of engraved line, whereas the Dutch plates are mostly etched, and have a softer and more 'artistic' quality. Whether or not it was cheaper to have plates made in Holland, which at that time was the principal centre for European printmaking, is not certain, but the cost of manufacturing copper plates in either country was high. The

Above: *Etching a copper plate, from Bosse.*
Below: *Using the echoppe, from Bosse.*
Right: *A 17th-century printmaking workshop engraved by Abraham Bosse. Hunterian Art Gallery, University of Glasgow.*

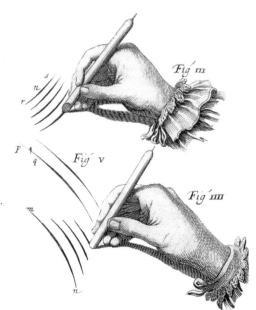

engraving of the plates for the *Theatrum Scotiae* cost £4.10 per plate[5] – the equivalent of three months' pay for one of Slezer's own gunners.

The printmaker engraving or etching his copper plate had, of course, to work from a drawing. A drawing made specifically to be engraved usually has two special features. Firstly, the drawing is the same size as the finished print (the engraver has enough problems transferring the design to the copper plate without having to alter the scale at the same time); secondly, most designs for engraving are finished in a monochrome wash, usually over an ink or pencil outline. The engraver would interpret these washes in engraved or etched lines.

Few of the drawings from which the *Theatrum Scotiae* plates were directly engraved have survived, but there are three such drawings preserved in the Ashmolean Museum in Oxford.[6] These drawings are not only the same size as the finished plates, but have been 'squared up': that is, a grid of squares has been ruled onto the drawing to assist in the transfer of the subject onto an identically squared copper plate. The sky has not been squared, as this part of the design could be left to the engraver to finish off. In one of these drawings the gridlines have even been numbered to assist the engraver.

Top: *A London-style engraved plate.* Above: *A Dutch-style engraved/etched plate.* Below: *Preliminary drawing for a Glasgow plate, with grid numbers just visible above bridge. Ashmolean Museum.*

The prospects which make up Slezer's *Theatrum Scotiae* fall into two general categories: views of towns from a distance, and close-ups of particular buildings or sets of buildings. The most obvious model for topographical prospects is to be found in the work of Wenceslaus Hollar, who was working in the generation before Slezer. Hollar's prints tend to be longer and thinner than Slezer's drawings, which are themselves closer to Hollar's format than the published plates.

Left: *Detail of St Andrews Cathedral. (SL.14)*
Right: *Same detail today.*

The published prospects are full of inconsistencies: on the one hand they can be extremely accurate, almost photographic, and on the other they are sometimes poorly drawn and badly put together. The most likely explanation for this is that they were made with the assistance of an optical device – the camera obscura, which projected a scene onto a flat surface. Certain evidence immediately supports such a conclusion: the pin-point accuracy of some parts of the prospects when viewed from the same spot today, the standard size of the drawings (possibly the size of a drawing screen), and the piecemeal arrangement of elements in some of the prospects.

The camera obscura was not a new invention in Slezer's day. The pin-hole camera effect had been known for centuries, and developments in optics had added refinements, like the scioptic ball, a device which had been invented earlier in the century, and which, when inserted in the shutters of a darkened room, projected a picture of the outside world onto the far wall. In London, after the restoration of the Monarchy, science received a boost from the patronage of Charles II, who gave his support to the founding of the Royal Observatory at Greenwich and the Royal Society, where Robert Hooke described a portable camera obscura to the members in 1694.

The pin-hole camera effect.

The camera obscura had been improved by combining a lens and a mirror, thus enabling the viewer to see the subject for the first time both the right way up and the right way round, a great improvement on the earlier versions where the pin-hole effect gave an image not only upside down but reversed left to right. Two types of camera obscura were available in Slezer's day. One consisted of a sort of pointed tent in which the viewer sat to make a drawing. A mirror reflected the view through a lens at the top which projected the scene onto a table. (Smaller versions could be used on a table top.) The second type, the 'box' camera obscura, had a lens in front and a mirror inside the box which reflected the image onto a viewing screen at the back. The observer would cover his head and the back of the box with a light-proof cloth.

The close-up views of buildings, especially in those cases where it is still possible to find the exact spot where the camera was set up, provide clues as to which of the two types of camera obscura Slezer may have used. With the box type, one would expect the eye level to be rather low, much closer to that of an artist sitting down to make a sketch, whereas with the tent type of camera, even a table-top one, the eye level would be similar to, or higher than, that of a viewer standing up.

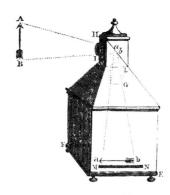

Most of Slezer's prospects were taken from a distance, from high points or rising ground, so the evidence is inconclusive, but in a few prospects, such as Roslin Chapel, where the point of view is both near and clear, the perspective of the pillars just inside the door indicates that the eye level is fairly high. Similar high viewpoints are discernible in a few of the other prospects, including that of Melrose Abbey.

The two types of camera obscura.

Evidence of the construction of prospects from the combination of a number of drawings can be found in the prints of Dryburgh, Melrose, and St Andrews Cathedral. By studying the perspective of the prospect at the actual site, it can be deduced that the plate showing the Ruins of Dryburgh Abbey, for example, must have been made up from at least two different drawings, one taken from the arch at the west end of the Abbey Church, and the other from a point on the south side. These two elements have been combined to create an impression of the interior of the ruins. The Melrose plate is even more strange, as the surviving wall of the central tower has been moved from the west (where it still survives today) to the south.

The plate of the ruins of the Cathedral of St Andrews, another of the ecclesiastical prospects, shows a different aspect of this 'cut and paste' technique. The ruins are all depicted accurately as seen from one single

Left: *Melrose Abbey. (SL.52)*
Right: *Melrose Abbey today.*

Rudera Ecclesiæ Cathedralis Sancti ANDREÆ. The Ruins of the Cathedrall of St ANDREWS.

St Andrews Cathedral. (SL.14)

A 'box' camera obscura in use, detail from Paul Sandby's Roslin Castle (c. 1775). Yale Center for British Art, Paul Mellon Collection.

spot within the site, but the span of the prospect is far wider than can comfortably be seen. Slezer again took two or more drawings, this time from the same spot, and combined them to make up the prospect. Similarly, in the plate of Crossraguel, where most of the buildings have been taken from one point, the west perimeter wall with its terminal doocot has been observed from quite a different angle and squashed into the composition, giving a more compact picture of the ruins.

The paper of two of the final-stage Ashmolean drawings has been cut and pasted. The drawing of Glasgow Cathedral is made up of three pieces of paper, with the largest, holding the Cathedral, its Palace and the spires of the City, having been added to at the bottom and at the left. The drawing of Hamilton has also had a strip added to the top of the composition in order to make the drawing up to the size of the plate. A more experienced or accomplished artist would have used different techniques to harmonise the composition of the prospects, but Slezer is not, in that sense, an 'artist' but a surveyor or delineator of prospects. The camera obscura did not become a popular tool until well into the eighteenth century, so Slezer's apparent employment of it for his prospects of Scotland in the late seventeenth century is a remarkably early example of its use.

There can be no doubt that the *Theatrum Scotiae* was Slezer's own personal project, and that he was directly responsible for its production; nor are his skills as a draughtsman in doubt, since his maps and plans, both military and civilian, are of a consistently high standard. But the degree to which other artists were involved in his project – especially at the drawing stage – still remains a matter of speculation. We know from his own writings that he employed at least one other artist on the drawings for the *Theatrum Scotiae*, and some of the prospects, especially those which diverge from the standard pattern, may well be the work of others.

In a submission to the Scots Parliament he lists among his costs:

> *For bringing over a Painter, his charges to travel from place to place, and for drawing these 57 draughts contained in the said Theatrum Scotiae, at 2 lib. sterlin per draught,*
>
> £0114:00:00[7]

This might imply that Slezer had employed another artist to make all the prospects, but it has always been assumed that Slezer is here referring to himself, charging a second time for journeys already made on official business. Slezer was usually meticulous in reclaiming any financial outlay, and it would have been uncharacteristic of him not to name any artist who drew the prospects, when he named John Wyck, who provided the figures for them.

Slezer lists Wyck's payment along with the costs of finishing the draughts for engraving.

> *Item. To Mr Wycke, the battell painter at London, for touching and filling up the said 57 draughts with little figures, at 10 shillings sterlin per piece, inde* 0028:10:00[8]

John (or Jan) Wyck, known to his contemporaries as the 'battle painter' because of his prolific production of military scenes, also supplied illustrations to books such as Richard Blome's *The Gentlemans Recreation* (1686), a guide to the pleasures of hunting, shooting and fishing, whose illustrations contain many figures very much in the style of those in the prospects.

Given Wyck's involvement in the production of the plates, it is not surprising that the three full-size preparatory drawings at the Ashmolean Museum were attributed to him. Whether Wyck redrew the entire prospect, adding in the figures, or added them to an already finished drawing, cannot be deduced from the surviving examples, but some of the figures in the final engravings are so much out of scale with the buildings that a cut-and-paste technique (a perfectly legitimate seventeenth-century art practice) was probably used. Many of the figures in the plates are very similar: a gentleman sitting while another stands alongside, resting on a stick or pointing, seems to be a favourite. In one print, however, some of the figures are taken directly from the Falkland Palace plate where the man

Jan Wyck and his father (inset), engraving by Bannerman. Author's Collection.

walking to the left in the centre of the composition, and the two dogs, are used unchanged on the right of the Dalkeith plate, as are the two figures shaking hands.

Some of the prospects, especially those more ambitious perspectives intended for the volumes which were to have followed the *Theatrum Scotiae*, might well have been commissioned by Slezer from other artists, and a few plates, such as the perspectives of Heriot's Hospital and the College of Glasgow, are altogether different from the simple prospects which make up the majority of the plates in the *Theatrum Scotiae*. These two plates are similar in concept to Loggan's Oxford and Cambridge Plates, and an entry in one of the notebooks of George Vertue, made in the early eighteenth century, states in relation to Loggan that:

> One Kickers drew the views. & draughts of the Colleges of Oxford & those of Cambridge in partnership with him: & they both went to Scotland & there he drew the views in Theatrum Scotiae.[9]

The Kickers of the note is probably the artist Kickius, an accomplished topographical artist from the Netherlands, who, like both Slezer and John

A plate from Loggan's Oxania Illustrata *(1675).*

Wyck, had also been in the employ of the Duke of Lauderdale. George Vertue, though here writing a generation after these events, is generally a reliable recorder of information, but the majority of the engravings for the *Theatrum Scotiae* are of a very different order from the Loggan Oxford and Cambridge plates. Another artist with a more direct interest in the *Theatrum Scotiae* was Loggan's pupil, Robert White, the engraver, who was also a considerable artist in his own right. Although White specialised in portraiture, he did make a few topographical studies, and in Slezer's accounts given to Parliament in September 1696 he mentions one item:

> *The perspective of the insyde of the Abbay Church, with the stalls of the Knights of the Thistle, tuice drawn, once in Scotland, and the other by Mr Whyte at London,* £007:00:00[10]

This prospect was eventually engraved by Mazel and appears in the *Vitruvius Scoticus* of William Adam, where the drawing is attributed to John Wyck.

Robert White was the engraver in overall charge of the plates for the *Theatrum Scotiae*. Many of them were contracted out to engravers in Holland, probably in an attempt to minimise costs. Slezer was unfortunate in losing twelve of his copper plates at sea, sometime before publication, but most of the plates were shipped back safely to London for printing. Almost all of the plates are unsigned, but the signature of one of the Dutch printmakers does appear in plate 22 (Coast of Lothian) where 'Joh van den Avele fecit' can clearly be read on the road in the right of the plate. Avele also signed plate 28 (Hamilton). This printmaker had also signed plates 8 and 35 (Alloa and Scone), but the signatures have been deliberately erased. Strangely, these erased signatures are more easily detected on later impressions of the prints: both read 'J Avele fecit & aquaforti'. Van den Avele was a resident of Leiden, an etcher and engraver, who moved to Sweden in 1698 where he worked on a similar project to Slezer's – Count Eric Dahlberg's *Suecia antiqua et hodierna*, which was completed in 1714. It is difficult to understand why, or by whom, these signatures were removed, and there may well have been signatures on other plates. One possibility might be that White was trying to pass Dutch plates off as made in London. Curiously, Slezer later made a positive feature of their Dutch origin – but only after the accession of Mary and William of Orange. The only signed London-made plates bear White's name, but neither was used in the first edition of the *Theatrum Scotiae* in 1693.

If the practicalities of producing the copper plates for the *Theatrum Scotiae* were complex, the actual business of printing and publishing the volume

Robert White, engraving by Worthington. Author's Collection.

was not without its own difficulties. Slezer's plans for publication were well advanced when political turmoil endangered not only his literary ambitions but his own safety. On the death of Charles II, his brother James succeeded as James II and VII. As he was a Roman Catholic, this posed political problems, which culminated in the Revolution of 1688. William of Orange landed at Torbay on 5 November with a massive army, forcing the King to flee the country on 22 December. Slezer, now Captain of the Artillery Train, was an important military figure in Scotland. He had marched the Artillery Train to Carlisle in support of King James, and on his return to Edinburgh, where his old commander, the Duke of Gordon, was holding the Castle for King James, he was asked by the Estates of Parliament to swear allegiance to them. Having already sworn allegiance to James VII, he refused, and was imprisoned in the Canongate Tolbooth. In the April of that year, however, William and Mary (already King and Queen of England) were proclaimed King and Queen of Scotland, and after declaring his acceptance of the new order Slezer was released from imprisonment on 3 June 1689. He travelled down to London to see William III, whom he already knew from his Dutch trip of 1681, and was reinstated by him as Captain of the Artillery.

During this time Slezer also had problems with the text of the *Theatrum Scotiae*. It was originally intended to print a description in Latin to complement each plate. Slezer had approached the Geographer Royal, Sir Robert Sibbald, who had extracted entries from his 'Scotia Antiqua et Moderna'. These survive in manuscript in the National Library of Scotland, where each entry is double signed by Slezer and Sibbald. In the event, Slezer published the text translated into English without any mention of Sibbald and with no acknowledgement of any kind to him. It is possible that after the grant of the royal licence in 1693 Slezer felt that he had no need to involve the Geographer Royal and was safe to publish a book which would, under normal circumstances, have come under the Geographer Royal's virtual monopoly of matters Geographical in Scotland, but it is equally likely that Sibbald's brief conversion to Catholicism, which barred him from public office and put his life in danger from the mob, may have caused Slezer to excise his name from the book as undesirable in the new political climate.

Despite a flourishing publishing trade in Edinburgh, Slezer arranged for his book to be printed and published in London, and shortly after his own rehabilitation he returned there to supervise the production of the *Theatrum Scotiae*. He had one hundred copies printed on 'fine paper' and twenty-five copies printed on 'larger and finer paper'(effectively thicker). Both the text and the plates were printed on Royal size paper (508 × 635mm). The plates vary slightly but are around 230 × 415mm. Though it would have been possible to print two plates on one sheet if they had been bound vertically, each plate was printed on a single sheet which was folded in the centre and hinged into the book. It must be said, however, that the publication was not a success, and three years later Slezer was complaining to the Scots Parliament that he had still

> *near ane hundred of them lying on his hand at London, which do not sell, becaus the work is imperfect.*[11]

He also complains that the London booksellers 'do malitiously oppose the sale of this above mentioned Theatrum Scotiae',[12] which might account for his holding the entire stock himself.

Life after publication

The lack of success which met the publication of the *Theatrum Scotiae* did not, however, deter Slezer from his attempts to produce the other volumes promised in his foreword, and permitted under his royal licence. He petitioned Parliament in 1695 and, after the examination of his case, was granted a share in the proceeds of the Tunnage Act passed that year.

In the event, Slezer received very little money from this tax, and from the passing of the Tunnage Act until his death in 1717 he was never able to obtain the support he had been promised by Parliament, despite a series of court cases and petitions. His debts were made worse by the irregular payment of his own army salary and his inability to obtain reimbursement for his expenditure on the Artillery Train, for which he had provided

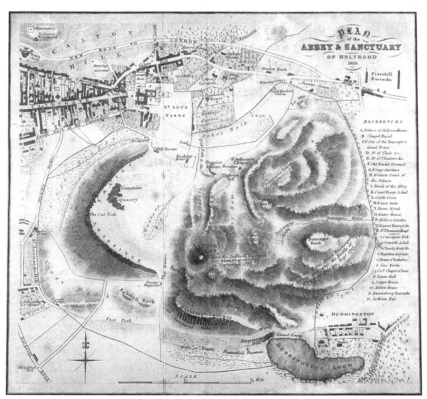

Plan of Holyrood sanctuary, engraving by J. Petrie (1819). Author's Collection.

uniforms using his own credit. This ultimately forced Slezer to seek shelter in the debtor's sanctuary of Holyrood.

Since the time of the original Abbey at Holyrood the Abbey bounds (which included the area of the King's Park) had been a place of sanctuary, particularly for those in danger of arrest for debt. This was not quite as restricting as being in prison: Slezer could live there through the week, and on Sunday he was free to visit his family in the city. Surprisingly, this confinement did not curtail his military activities as he was protected from the law when on active duty, and he remained Captain of the Artillery Train of Scotland (subsequently of North Britain) until its complete reorganisation in 1716. When the Royal Regiment of Artillery was formed, Slezer, along with most of the old Scottish Artillery Train, was placed on the sinking establishment, which meant that although he kept his rank and pay, his post was technically redundant. The Master-General did not have to wait long for the Captain's position to become vacant, however, for John Slezer died, still living in the sanctuary of the Abbey bounds, in 1717, leaving debts of over £2000. It was not until 1723 that the Army settled all of Slezer's debts, and paid the surplus, some £83 sterling, to his surviving son Charles, a soldier who had by this time fought on the Continent under the Duke of Marlborough.

The THEATRUM SCOTIAE

The first edition of the *Theatrum Scotiae*, the only edition produced under the direct supervision of Slezer, was published in 1693. The book was the product of a collaboration between Slezer and the Geographer Royal, Sir Robert Sibbald. It is not certain how early their collaboration started, but by 1691 both had signed a contract, which is no longer extant, for the production of the book.[13] Sibbald was to furnish the text for the *Theatrum Scotiae*, and this was to consist of descriptions of the places featured in the plates. Sibbald extracted the entries from his 'Scotia Antiqua et Moderna'. The entries were mainly antiquarian in content, and reflected Sibbald's own interest in the derivation of placenames and the Roman occupation of Scotland. The text was to have been printed in Latin, which Sibbald preferred to write in, but Slezer had the entries translated and printed in English. This may reflect the new scientific popularism as promoted by the Royal Society in London, at the instigation of Samuel Pepys. One Latin portion of the text did, however, survive – the poems on Scottish towns by Arthur and John Johnston.

Slezer also tried to court the favour of the Scots nobility by dedicating the entries to potential patrons. These dedications were accompanied by engravings of the coats of arms of the dedicatees. The coats of arms were never reprinted in subsequent editions, and in 1718, when the plates were reissued after Slezer's death, long-winded dedications to a new set of leading figures were engraved directly on the plates. These new dedications reflect the political changes after 1715.

A number of early manuscripts in the National Library of Scotland show something of the changes which the book underwent before its first publication in 1693. One is the original agreed text of the Slezer-Sibbald collaboration mentioned above.[14] Written entirely in Latin, it has a full foreword by Sibbald and contains the descriptive entries for each of the places covered by the plates. Each description is signed by both Sibbald and Slezer, and this double signing of the entries attests both to its importance, and perhaps to a growing distrust between the two parties. This manuscript text differs from the final version of the *Theatrum Scotiae* in some respects:

Sir Robert Sibbald, engraving by Lizars.

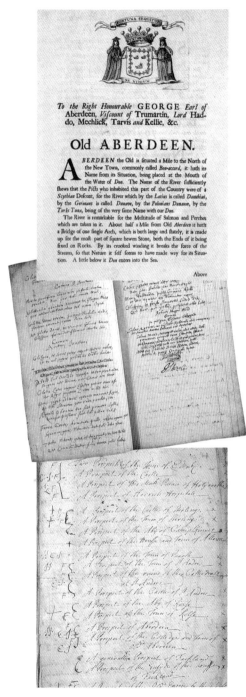

Top: *Typical text page from the first edition of the* Theatrum Scotiae *(1693).*
Middle: *Sibbald and Slezer's manuscript text.*
Bottom: *The List of Prospects.*

there are a number of places described which do not appear in the book as published, including a few private houses such as Thirlestane and Glamis. Slezer was confident he would be able to publish these in the next volume, where private houses were to be a specific feature. Other omissions include the Abbeys of Pluscardine, Cambuskenneth, and Inchcolm, together with the town of Kilsyth and the Castle of Blackness. It is possible that these may have been amongst the twelve plates which were lost at sea before the 1693 publication.

Another manuscript preserved in the National Library of Scotland[15] represents a slightly earlier stage of the development of the *Theatrum Scotiae*. This document is a list of prospects, headed 'Prospects and Antiquities of Scotland', probably written in Slezer's own hand and annotated by Sir Robert Sibbald with details of the Latin epigrams which he was inserting in the text. This list is very close to the published format of the book (even closer to the manuscript text), but differs in a number of details. The two prospects of Edinburgh are given, with the additional prospects of the Palace of Holyroodhouse, the Castle, and Heriot's Hospital. (The two latter were eventually engraved but do not appear in the 1693 edition.) Other prospects listed which do not appear in the first edition are Kilsyth, Blackness Castle, and the Abbeys of Brechin, Inchcolm, Pluscardine, and Kinloss. A further section consists of private houses: two prospects of Thirlestane Castle, Glamis, and Hatton House (all four were engraved) and Castle Lyon (which was not engraved). Most of these places are included in the full Slezer-Sibbald manuscript.

The descriptions of some of the prospects differ interestingly from the final engraved titles. Hamilton is described as 'The Housse and Toun of Hammilton', and Haddington as 'The Church and Toun of Haddingtoun' – both much more descriptive of the plates. The titles of the two Dryburgh prospects are likewise 'A Generall Prospect of Dryborrough' and 'A Particular Prospect of the Ruins of the Aby of Dryborrough', both more descriptive and accurate than the titles found on the plates. A similar loss of clarity is found in the change from 'A Prospect of the Bass from the Castle of Tamtanneld' (Tantallon) to 'The Prospect of Ye Bass from Ye South shore'. This list also uses the modern form of Arbroath. All these are slight differences, but the use in the title of 'Prospects and Antiquities' gives a clearer indication of Slezer's overall concept of a book depicting the nation both past and present.

The Plates of the
Theatrum Scotiae

Edinburgh

Facies Arcis EDENBURGEENÆ *The Southside of the* Castle *of* EDINBURGH.

*The Southside of the Castle of
Edinburgh. (SL.1)*

Previous page.

The Southside of the Castle of Edinburgh. (SL.1)

Edinburgh Castle from the south, including the town and Heriot's Hospital. The Castle is seen on the left of the print, and below it are the roofs of Portsburgh. Between Heriot's Hospital and the Castle are the roofs of the houses surrounding the Grassmarket and the houses on the south-west of the Old Town. St Giles dominates, but the spires of both the Tron Church, the Chapel of St Mary Magdalene, and the square tower of the Greyfriars Church also feature. Below St Giles, and framed by it and the tower of the Tron, is the old Parliament House, projecting out over the surrounding houses. At the extreme right of the print, Heriot's Hospital is set within the protection of the Telfer Wall, and, forming part of this wall between the tower of St Mary Magdalene and that of Greyfriars, can be seen the 'tower in the vennel' which marks the junction with the old Flodden Wall.

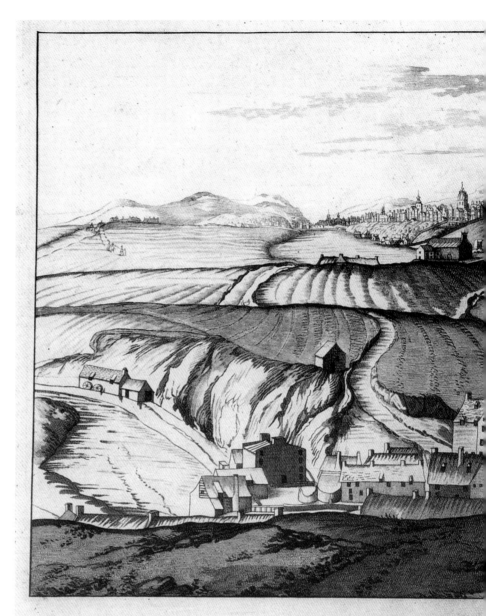

Prospectus Civitatis EDINBURGENÆ a prædio

dicto. The Prospect of EDINBRUGH from ỹ DEAN.

2.

The Prospect of Edinburgh from Ye Dean. (SL.2)

The view of the City of Edinburgh from the north-west shows the Village of Dean in the foreground. A prominent feature of this view is the North (or Nor') Loch which protected the city on its northern side, and at the near end of which can be seen old St Cuthbert's Church below the Castle. Heriot's Hospital can be seen just to the right of the Castle rock, and the line of the High Street can be traced by the spires of St Giles, the Tron Church, the Netherbow Port, and, in the Canongate, the Tolbooth and the Chapel Royal of the Palace of Holyrood in the distance. Below Calton Hill, at the far end of the North Loch, is the unfinished Church of Trinity College at the top of the Leith Wynd.

The North-East View of Edinburgh Castle. (SL.59)

The north-east view of the Castle was not published in the first edition of the Theatrum Scotiae. *This close-up view of the Castle is similar to the drawing of the Castle in 1675, but with the addition of a fortified area in front of the main gate. Below the Castle, on the left of the plate, is the suburb of Portsburgh, outside the main walls of the city and accessed by the West Port.*

The North-East View of EDINBURGH CASTLE.

Dumbarton

The Castle of Dumbritton from Kilpatrick. (SL.3)

Dumbarton Castle in the distance, as seen from Kilpatrick. Dumbarton Rock is much distorted in this prospect, looking down the Clyde from Kilpatrick.

Arx BRITANNODUNENSIS ab Oppido Cella Patricij dicto. The Castle of DUMBRITTON from Kilpatrick.

Prospectus Arcis Regiæ BRITANNODUNENSIS ab Occidente. Their Ma.ties Castle of DUMBRITTON from the West

Their Ma'ties Castle of Dumbritton from the West. (SL.4)

These plates show Dumbarton Castle from the town side, showing the Wallace Tower, and from the Clyde. Dumbarton was the most important fortress on the west coast of Scotland. Set on a rock guarded by the rivers Leven and Clyde, it had superb natural defences.

The Prospect of Ye Castle of Dumbritton from ye East. (SL.5)

Facies Arcis BRITANNODUNENSIS ab Oriente. The Prospect of ỹ Castle of DUMBRITTON from ỹ East

The Prospect of the Town of Sterling from the East.   URI

TERLINI, PROSPECTUS AB ORIENTE.

Stirling

The Prospect of the Town of Sterling from the East. (SL.6)

This shows Stirling from the east. The Castle dominates the town from the top of the hill and guards the old bridge, which can be seen on the right. The ruins in the foreground are of the Abbey of Cambuskenneth, but its most celebrated surviving building, the tower, is not depicted.

*The Prospect of their Ma'ties
Castle of Sterling. (SL.7)*

*The titling on this plate has been
changed from 'His Ma'ties' to
'their Ma'ties' due to the accession
of William and Mary. A drawing
of this view by Slezer is preserved
in the Public Record Office
in London.*

The Prospect of their Maties *Castle of Sterling.* | ARCIS REGIÆ STERLINENSIS PROSPECTUS.

7.

*The Prospect of Her Ma:ties
Castle of Sterling. (SL.60)*

*This engraving of Stirling, which
was not used in the first edition
of the* Theatrum Scotiae, *shows
the Castle from a vantage point
on a high rock in the present-day
graveyard to the east of the Castle.
The elaborate gatehouse which
formed such a decorative feature of
Stirling Castle was reconstructed in
the eighteenth century.*

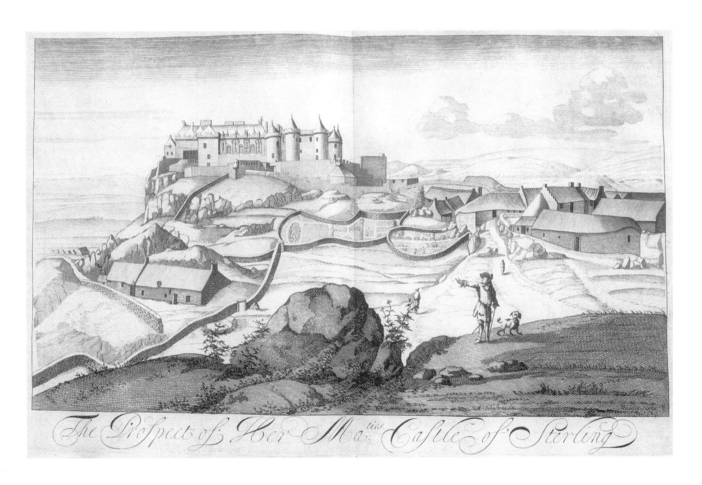

The Prospect of Her Ma.ties Castle of Sterling

Alloa

The Prospect of the House & of the Town of Alloua. (SL.8)

Alloa is one of the towns very much changed from Slezer's day. The castellated tower and surrounding buildings are Alloa House.

The Prospect of the House, & of the Town of Alloua. PROSPECTUS ARCIS, ET OPPIDI DE ALLOA.

Linlithgow

The Prospect of the Town of Linlithgow. (SL.9)

This plate shows Linlithgow from a hill to the south of the town, just above the present-day canal. The beehive doocot to be seen on the left foreground of the town still survives.

Prospectus Civitatis LIMNUCHI. The Prospect of the Town of LINLITHGOW.

The Prospect of Their Maj'ties Palace of Linlithgow. (SL.10)

This prospect of Linlithgow Palace was taken from the west side of the loch. The Palace was burned in 1745 and never refurbished. St Michael's Church, which shares the Palace site, had the beautiful crown on its tower removed in the nineteenth century.

Prospectus Regis Palatis LIMNUCHENSIS. The Prospect of Their Maj.ties Palace of LINLITHGOW.

10.

Falkland Palace

*The Prospect of Falkland from the
East. (SL.11)*

*Falkland Palace was formerly one
of the seats of the Thanes of Fife
and later forfeited to the crown.*

Prospectus FALCOLANDIÆ ab Oriente. The Prospect of FALKLAND from the East.

Palace of Falkland. (SL.12)

*In this interior prospect the scale of the buildings and the scale of the figures is very much at odds, the figures being much too small for the courtyard which they inhabit.
The east wing (on the left) burnt down in the reign of Charles II, and though depicted as complete in this prospect, it was probably already ruinous, as can be seen in the view from the east.*

St Andrews

The Prospect of the Town of St Andrews. (SL.13)

This general prospect of St Andrews was taken from the Kinkell Braes to the south of the city, showing the harbour and the great Cathedral within its encircling walls, which remain little changed today. The tower in the centre of the plate is that of St Salvator's College, while that to the left belongs to Holy Trinity, the parish church of the town.

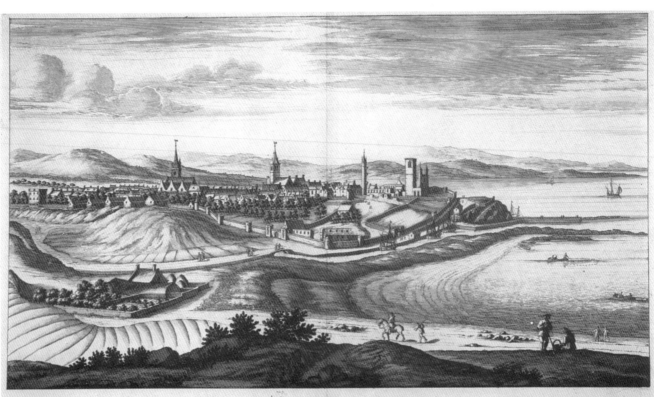

Faeics Guitatis Sancti ANDREÆ: *The Prospect of The Town of* St ANDREWS.

Rudera Ecclesiæ Cathedralis Sancti ANDREÆ.   The Ruins of the Cathedrall of St ANDREWS.

The Ruins of the Cathedrall of St Andrews. (SL.14)

These plates show the remains of St Andrews Cathedral, with the great tower of the Church of St Rule, and the remains of the Castle of St Andrews which served as the palace of the Archbishop. It was in this building in 1546 that Cardinal Beaton was murdered.

The Ruins of the Castle of St Andrews. (SL.15)

Rudera Arcis Sancti ANDREÆ.   The Ruins of the Castle of St ANDREWS.

31

Facies Civitatis GLASGOW ab Oriente Estevo. The Pros

Glasgow

*The Prospect of ye Town
of Glasgow from ye North
East. (SL.16)*

*This prospect was taken from
the high ground to the east of
Glasgow Cathedral. Just beyond
the Cathedral is the Castle of the
Archbishop. In the distance are the
spires of the Tron, Old College,
Blackfriars and the Tolbooth.
In the foreground the bridge over
the Molendinar Burn leads into
the Drygate.*

of ÿ Town of GLASGOW from ÿ North East

17

Facies Civitatis GLASCOÆ ab Austro. The prospect of the Town of GLASGOW from ỹ South.

The prospect of the Town of
Glasgow from ye South. (SL.17)

This view of Glasgow is taken
from the south bank of the
river Clyde and shows the old
eight-arched bridge leading to
the Brigport. Beside this, on the
far bank, is the steeple of the
Merchants Hall, finished in 1665.
To the right of the prospect are a
cluster of spires: the farthest right
is that of the Cathedral, and the
other three are the Tolbooth, the
Old College of the University, and
the Church of the Blackfriars. The
steeple of the Tron Church can be
seen halfway between these and the
Merchants Hall.

The Colledge of Glasgow.
(SL.18)

The buildings of the University
of Glasgow are depicted with
the adjoining Blackfriars Church
and graveyard. The University
buildings survived until the
nineteenth century when they were
demolished to make way for more
modern buildings.

The COLLEDGE of GLASGOW

Aberdeen

New Aberdene from the Block house. (SL.19)

This plate shows the two separate towns of Old and New Aberdeen, seen from the mouth of the river Dee. The blockhouse of the title is the round building on the other side of the river. On the extreme right can be seen the tower and twin spires of St Machar's Cathedral.

Facies Civitatis Novæ ABREDONIÆ ut a propugnaculo Blockhous dito aspicitur. New ABERDENE from the Block houses.

*The Prospect of Old Aberdien.
(SL.20)*

*Here, the town of Old Aberdeen
is seen from the south. Part
of the long High Street can be
seen in the centre of the built-up
area, and St Machar's Cathedral
dominates the far end of the town.
In the centre, the set of buildings
with the crowned tower are the
King's College.*

Facies Ciuitætis ABERDONIÆ Veteris. The Prospect of Old ABERDIEN.

Haddington

*The Prospect of the Town of
Haddingtown. (SL.21)*

*This prospect shows the Church
of St Mary at Haddington, known
as the 'Lamp of the Lothians',
seen from the south. The mill to
the extreme left of the plate still
exists, and is now an arts centre.
The bridge and some of the houses
on the right of the plate are little
changed, and the wall which
surrounds the graveyard can still
be traced. On the far side of the
ruined choir of the Church is the
Lauderdale Aisle where John,
Duke of Lauderdale, Slezer's
patron, was buried.*

Prospectus Civitatis HADINÆ.   *The Prospect of the Town of* HADDINGTOWN.

Musselburgh

The Coast of Lothian from Stony hill. (SL.22)

The plate of the Coast of Lothian shows the town of Musselburgh and is so named in the original drawing. To the left of the town is the suburb of Fisherrow and on the right of the plate the Church of Inveresk. The main features within the town are Pinkie House and the tower of the Tolbooth. In the distance lie Prestonpans, Longniddry, and, on the horizon, North Berwick Law and the Bass Rock. Stonyhill borders on the grounds of Brunstane House, which Slezer depicted in one of his estate plans.

Prospectus Oræ maritimæ LOTHIANÆ a Prædio de Stony hill. The Coast of LOTHIAN from Stony hill.

22.

Montrose

*The Prospect of the town of
Montrose. (SL.23)*

*The prospect of Montrose is taken
from high ground to the west of
the town. The most prominent
landmarks are the Parish Church
which dominates the town, and,
a little to the right, the spire of
the Tolbooth. Farther right still,
on the eastern edge of the town,
is the windmill which gave the
name to Windmill Hill. In the
right foreground is Montrose basin,
and the channel which connects
it to the sea can be seen in the
middle distance.*

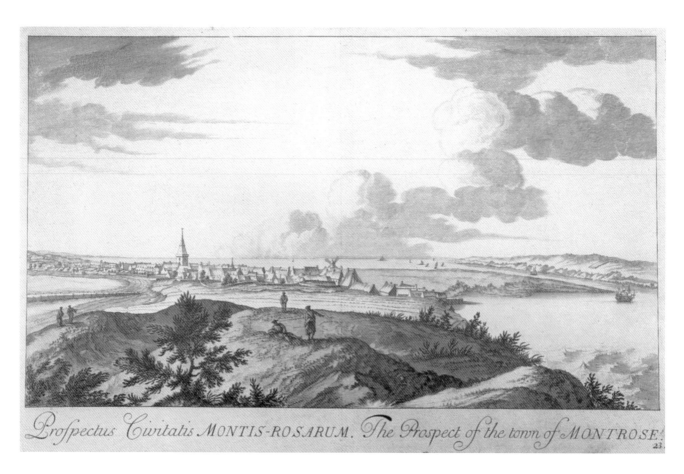

Prospectus Civitatis MONTIS-ROSARUM. The Prospect of the town of MONTROSE.

Prospectus Civitatis CALIDONIÆ . The Prospect of the Town of DUNKELD .

24

Dunkeld

The Prospect of the Town of Dunkeld. (SL.24)

This prospect shows the Cathedral Church of Dunkeld and the town from the east, with Dunkeld House (now demolished) in the centre. Slezer's viewpoint is perhaps more famous even than the town: it is the hill of Birnam.

The Cathedrall Church of Dunkell. (SL.25)

Ecclesia Cathedralis CALIDONIÆ . The Cathedrall Church of DUNKELL .

25

The close-up view of Dunkeld Cathedral was taken from the south, quite close to the building, as the riverbank is not far from the Cathedral on this side. The building remains in very much the same condition today.

Dunblane

The Prospect of the Town of Dumblane. (SL.26)

On the right of this plate is the old bridge over the river Allan. This prospect seems to have been taken during the harvest period, for grain is drying out in stooks.

Prospectus Oppidi Dumblani. The Prospect of the Town of Dumblane.

26.

The Cathedrall Church of Dumblane. (SL.27)

This view of Dunblane shows the remains of the Cathedral, which, unlike that at Dunkeld, has been rebuilt.

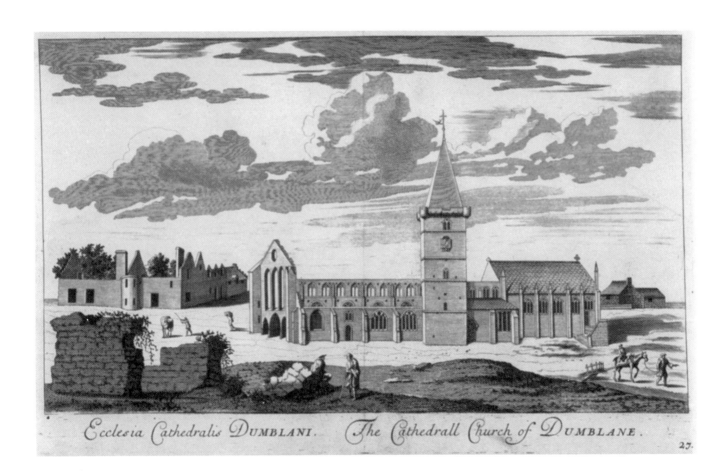

Ecclesia Cathedralis DUMBLANI.   *The Cathedrall Church of* DUMBLANE.   27.

Prospectus Oppidi Hamiltoniæ. The Pros

Hamilton

The Prospect of the Town of Hamilton. (SL.28)

This is another of the plates signed by the Dutch engraver Van den Avele. (The signature is placed within the image, directly below the nearest horseman.) Hamilton Palace, which is seen in the distance, was rebuilt shortly after Slezer made this prospect.

of the Town of HAMILTON.

28.

Ayr

*The Prospect of the Town of Air
from the East. (SL.29)*

*This view of the town of Ayr was
taken from the north-west, with
the Old Bridge on the extreme left,
the spire of the Tolbooth in the
centre, and on the right the tower
of the Church of St John, which
is the only part of the building to
survive today. To the far right
are the fortifications which guarded
the harbour.*

Prospectus Civitatis AERÆ ab Orientale. The Prospect of the Town of AIR from the East.

29

Prospectus Civitatis Aeræ a Domo de Newtown. The Town of Aire, from ÿ House of Newtowne.

30

The Town of Aire, from ye House
of Newtowne. (SL.30)

The Old Bridge which featured
on the extreme left of the previous
plate appears in the centre of this
prospect. The fortified building
on the right is the Castle of
Newtown, and the building by the
river on the centre left is the New
Church which replaced the ancient
Greyfriars.

Dunottar

The Prospect of Dunotter Castle (SL.31) (below) and the drawing on which it was based.

Dunottar was one of the first castles surveyed by Slezer as Chief Engineer. This prospect shows the Castle from the cliffs on the Stonehaven side. It was to Dunottar that the Honours of Scotland were sent during the Civil War. In the reign of Charles II, Dunottar was used as a prison for Covenanters, and during the Revolution of 1688-9 for suspected Jacobites. The buildings were dismantled in 1718, after the estates of the Earl Marischal were confiscated following the Jacobite rising of 1715.

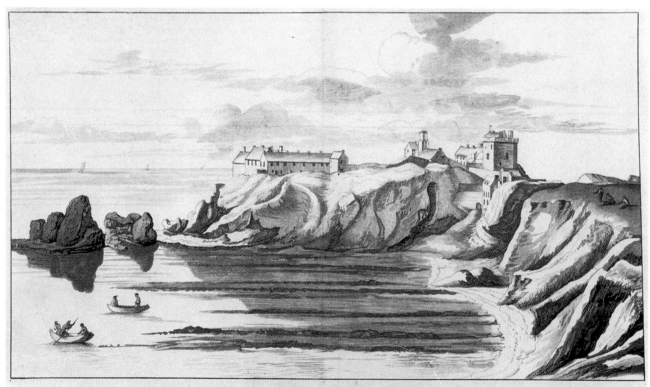

PROSPECTUS ARCIS DUNOTRIE. *The Prospect of* Dunotter Castle.

John Slezer, Plan of Dunottar (1675).

Dunottar today.

John Slezer, drawing of 'The Prospect of Dunotter from the foot of the brea opposite to the Entre'.

49

Dryburgh

*The Prospect of the Town of
Dryburgh. (SL.32)*

*Although described as the town
of Dryburgh, this is simply a
general view of the Abbey remains
with the river Tweed in the
foreground. It is described more
accurately in the manuscript list of
prospects as 'A Generall Prospect
of Dryborrough', and the more
detailed view (opposite) as 'A
Particular Prospect of the ruins of
the Aby of Dryborrough'.*[16]

Prospectus Oppidi de DRYBURGH. *The Prospect of the Town of* DRYBURGH.

32.

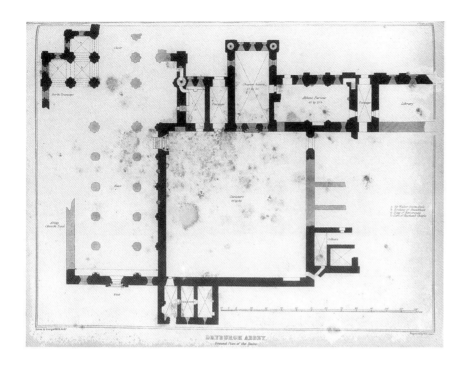

Plan of Dryburgh Abbey, from James Morton, Monastic Annals of Teviotdale *(Edinburgh, 1832).*

The Ruines of the Abbey of Drybrugh. (SL.33)

The plate of the ruins of Dryburgh Abbey contains the largest and most clearly costumed figures in the whole series. The vaults on the left were later to become the resting place of the remains of Sir Walter Scott. This prospect was made up from at least two separate drawings taken from different positions within the ruins.

Rudera Cænoby de DRYBRUGH. *The Ruines of the Abbey of* DRYBRUGH.

33.

Prospectus Civitatis INNERNESS. The prospect of ye Town of INNERNESS.

34.

Inverness

The prospect of ye Town of Innerness. (SL.34)

Inverness with its old Castle and, in Slezer's day, new seven-arched bridge is seen here from the north side of the river Ness.

Scone

The Prospect of the House and Town of Skuyn. (SL.35)

The old town was swept away to improve the estates of the Palace, which was completely rebuilt. The moot hill where Kings of Scotland were crowned appears to the right of the old Abbey gatehouse.

Prospectus Palaty et Oppidi de SKUYN. The Prospect of the House and Town of SKUYN.

35.

Prospectus Oppidi Elginæ. The Prospect of the Town of ELGINE.

36.

Elgin

The Prospect of the Town of Elgine. (SL.36)

This prospect shows Elgin from the north, with a bend of the river Lossie in the foreground. The ruins of the Cathedral are on the far left of the plate, with the bishop's lodging in front and the castle hill on the far right. In the centre of the plate is the roofed tower of the Church of St Giles (demolished in 1826). The flat tower to the right of St Giles is part of Thunderton House, built on the site of the Royal 'Great Lodging' in which Bonnie Prince Charlie stayed before the battle of Culloden which was fought nearby in 1746.

Rudera Templi Cathedralis ELGINI. The Ruins of the Cathedrall Church of ELGIN.

37.

The Ruins of the Cathedrall Church of Elgin. (SL.37)

53

Dundee

*The Prospect of ye Town of
Dundee. (SL.38)*

*The City of Dundee from the
north. Slezer was made a burgess
of Dundee in 1678.*

Prospectus Civitatis TAODUNI. The Prospect of ỹ Town of DUNDEE.

38.

*The Prospect of ye Town of
Dundee from ye East. (SL.39)*

*The plate of Dundee from the east
shows, in the foreground, women
washing and beating cloth.*

Prospectus Civitatis TAODUNI ab Oriente. The Prospect of ỹ Town of DUNDEE from ỹ East.

39·

Arbroath

*The Prospect of ye Town of
Aberbrothick. (SL.40)*

*This general view of Arbroath
was taken from the top of Dinland
Hill to the south of the town. The
remains of the Abbey are on the
left of the town and, following the
High Street down to the harbour,
the only other major building is
the Parish Church in the centre of
the plate. The small street in the
foreground is the Millgate, and on
the right of the plate one can see
the Lady Bridge with the roofs
of Marketgate beyond. Between
these two, and hidden by the rising
ground, is the suburb of Burnside
and the Shambles Bridge.*

Prospectus Oppidi Aberbrothiæ. The Prospect of ỹ Town of Aberbrothick.

40.

The Prospect of ye Abby of Aberbrothick. (SL.41)

The Theatrum Scotiae *uses the full Latinised version of the town's name, 'Aberbrothick', but in the early list of prospects Slezer uses the more modern form of Arbroath.*

Prospectus Cænobÿ ABERBROTHIÆ . The Prospect of ÿ Abby of ABERBROTHICK . 41.

57

Crossraguel

The Ruines of ye Abby of Corsregal. (SL.42)

The prospect of the ruins of the Abbey of Crossraguel was taken from the hill immediately to the south of the ruins. Like some of Slezer's other plates of ecclesiastical ruins, this prospect was made up from a number of drawings. The wall on the far left of the prospect, ending in a doocot, has been moved nearer to the viewer in order to make a neater picture.

Rudera Cænoby de CORSREGAL *seu crucis* Sᵗ *Reguli* *The Ruines of y̆ Abby of* CORSREGAL.

Fortrose

The Channery Town of Ross. (SL.43)

Fortrose was still a cathedral town and the seat of a bishop when Slezer made this, the farthest north of all the prospects. In the middle ground one can see clearly the run-rigs — cultivation in strips of land rather than in the enclosed fields we know today. On the far right of the town are agricultural buildings and ricks of hay or unthreshed corn.

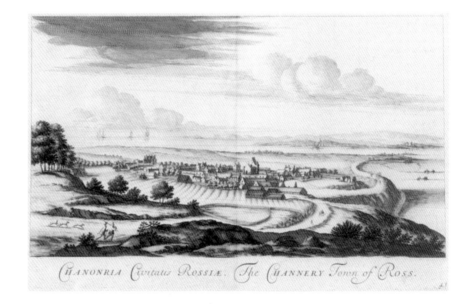

CHANONRIA *Civitatis* ROSSIÆ. *The* CHANNERY *Town of* ROSS.

Perth

The Prospect of ye Town of Perth. (SL.44)

Perth was a very important town in seventeenth-century Scotland, and one of the few places to provide Slezer with direct funding. Provost Hays gave Slezer the sum of £50 on the town's behalf towards his project. The prospect is dominated by the Church of St John. The ships at the south end of the town show Perth as a busy port at this time.

Prospectus Civitatis PERTHI. Th. Prospect of ye Town of PERTH.

Dunfermline

The Prospect of ye Town & Abby of Dumfermling. (SL.45)

This view of Dunfermline was taken from the ruins of Malcolm Canmore's tower to the west of the Abbey, and shows the remains of the Abbey Church and the ruins of the Palace buildings.

Prospectus Oppidi et Cænoby FERMELODUNENSIS The Prospect of y͞e Town & Abby of DUMFERMLING.

45.

*The Prospect of the Abby of
Dumfermling. (SL.46)*

*The view of Dunfermline from the
south shows very little of the town,
which was on the other side of the
Abbey lands. The prospect was
taken from a vantage point near
to Pittencrieff House, which was
built around the time Slezer made
this prospect.*

Prospectus Cenoby FERMELODUNENSIS. The Prospect of the Abby of DUMEERMLING.

Culross

*The Prospect of ye House &
Town of Colross. (SL.47)*

*Slezer's prospect of Culross was
made from a group of rocks in
the river Forth which are easily
accessible at low tide and still
survive today. The figures added
to this plate give a distorted idea
of the size of the rocks (they are
quite small). The Abbey ruins
and surviving Church dominate
the top of the hill, with Culross
House and its extensive gardens
to the right.*

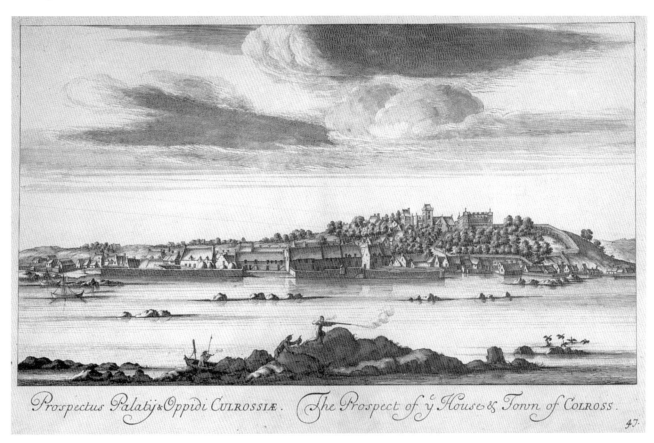

Prospectus Palatij & Oppidi CULROSSIÆ. *The Prospect of y̆ House & Town of* COLROSS.

47.

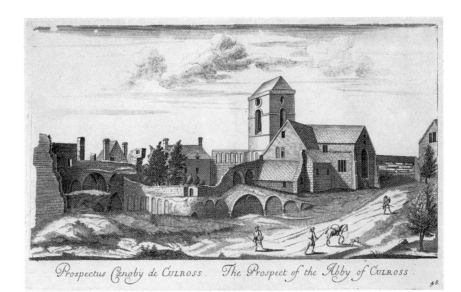

Prospectus Cœnobij de CULROSS. *The Prospect of the Abby of* CULROSS.

The Prospect of the Abby of Culross. (SL.48)

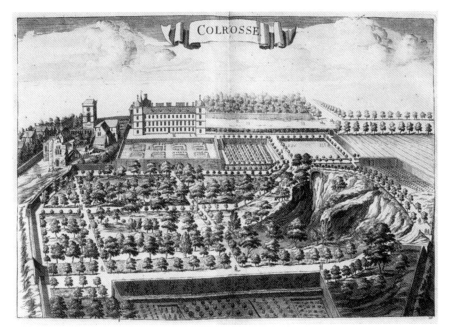

COLROSSE

Colrosse. (SL.69)

In the later editions of the Theatrum Scotiae, this plate of Culross House showing the extensive gardens in greater detail was issued. This plate was engraved in a more modern style using the full plate and with the titling on a ribbon within the image.

Kelso

The Prospect of the Town of Kelso. (SL.49)

This general view of Kelso was taken from the south side of the river Tweed, and the two roofs in the foreground are part of the village of Maxwellheugh. The Abbey ruins are situated above these and the cauld and Abbey mill (still a working mill today). The ferry seen in the centre of the plate was superseded by a bridge only in the eighteenth century. This prospect was probably made before the disastrous fire which destroyed most of the town in 1684. A map of the town made to survey the damage immediately after the fire is probably the work of Slezer, who would have been the ideal person to make a survey of the devastated town.

Prospectus Oppidi CALS

s. *The Prospect of the Town of* KELSO.

49.

The Abby of Kelso. (SL.50)

The plate of the Abbey shows the extent of its rebuilding for use as the parish church, and also shows the school building which was added to it in the seventeenth century.

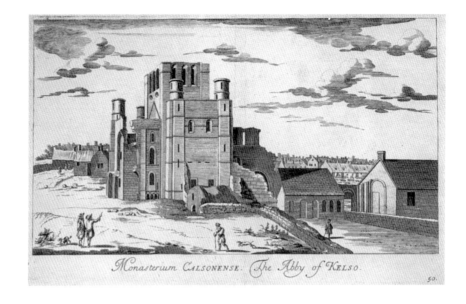

John Slezer, Map of Kelso in 1684. By permission of the Duke of Roxburghe.

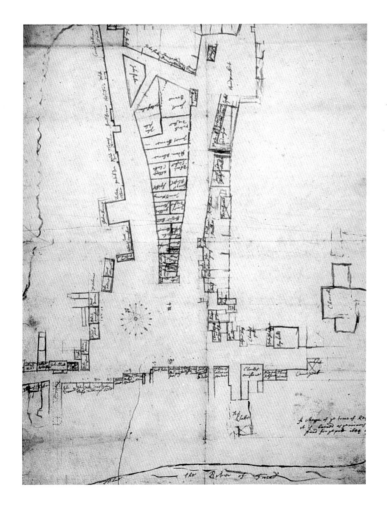

Bothwell

*The prospect of Bothwell
Castle. (SL.51)*

*Bothwell is the only castle to be
featured by Slezer which was
not a working fortification. This
is strange, given his interest in
Scotland's past and the fact that he
is known to have visited Tantallon
and must have seen the ruined
castles at Roxburgh and Dunbar.*

Prospectus Arcis BOTHWELIÆ. *The prospect of* BOTHWELL *Castle*.

51.

Melrose

The Ruines of the Abbie of Melross. (SL.52)

Melrose Abbey from the south. Melrose, like other Border Abbeys, suffered in the raid made by the Earl of Hertford in 1545. As at Kelso, part of the ruins were rebuilt for use as a parish church, and continued in this use until the early nineteenth century. Like that of Dryburgh, this prospect was made up from a number of drawings.

Rudera Cænoby de MELROSS, The Ruines of the Abbie of MELROSS. 52

Brechin

The Prospect of ye Towne of Brechin. (SL.53)

The prospect of Brechin was taken from high ground on the south bank of the river Southesk. The spire of the Cathedral Church is complemented by the eleventh-century round tower. Immediately in front of these, on the high riverbank, stands Brechin Castle. The buildings to the right, by the river, are mills, and the old bridge would be just off to the right.

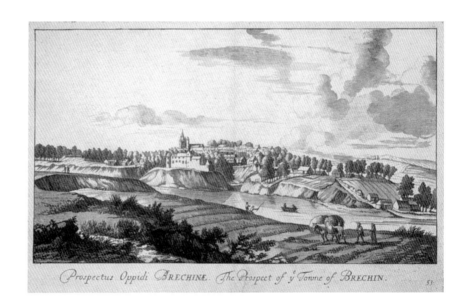

Prospectus Oppidi BRECHINE. The Prospect of y Towne of BRECHIN. 53

Roslin

The Chappell of Rosslin. (SL.54)

This prospect of Roslin Chapel was taken from the south-east corner of the present graveyard where the ground falls dramatically into the valley.

Capella de ROSSLIN. The Chappell of ROSSLIN. 54.

Paisley

The Prospect of the Abbey & town
of Paislay. (SL.55)

Paisley from the hill to the south.
The Abbey is the substantial
building to the right of the plate,
the Parish Church is in the centre,
beyond the bridge over the river
Cart. Paisley was numbered
57 on the copper plate, but
correctly numbered 55 in the table
of contents.

Prospectus Cœnobÿ et Civitatis PASLETI. The Prospect of the Abbey & town of PAISLAY.

57.

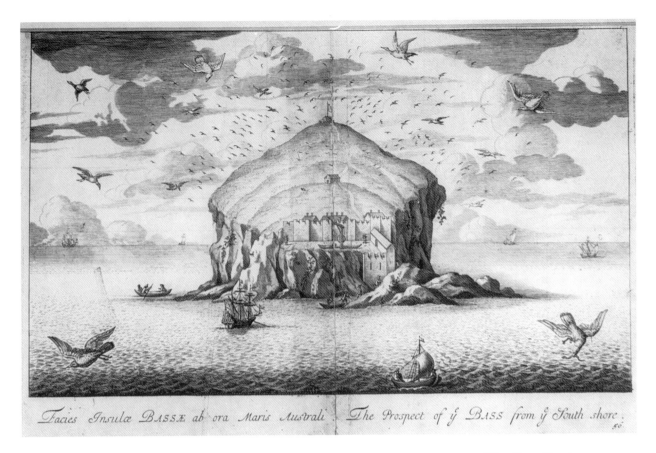

Facies Insulæ BASSÆ ab ora Maris Australi   The Prospect of ỹ BASS from ỹ South shore.

Latus Insulæ BASSÆ Orientale.   The East syde of the BASS.

The Bass Rock

The Prospect of ye Bass from ye South shore. (SL.56)

Of the two plates depicting the Bass Rock, that from the south shore is both the more familiar and the more accurate. In the list of prospects this view is described as a prospect from the castle of Tantallon. Tantallon can be seen on the shore in the other view.

The East syde of the Bass. (SL.57)

REPRESENTATION

For Captain JOHN SLEZER, *Anent the* History, *and* Present State *of* SCOTLAND *to be published by him.*

THe Captain, fince, and upon the Faith of, the *Act* of *Tunnage*, has fo far advanced his *Work*, that the Lords of His Majefties Privy Council has appointed a Committee of their own Number, to revife it : And hoping, the Work will give Satisfaction, both in the Defcription & Draughts, to all, who are Lovers of their Countrey, and of what is Curious and Diverting, he humbly offers an View of the Work it felf, and of the Contents of it, to *His Majefties High Commiffioner*, and the Right Honourable the *Eftates of Parliament*.

The Work is to be Printed upon Paper of the fame Size and Fynnefs, with the *Title Page* ; and the *FIRST VOLUME* confifts of *Two Parts* : In the *Firft* of which, are thefe following Chapters.

1. Of *BRITTAIN* in general.
2. Of *SCOTLAND* in general.
3. Of the *WALLS* built by the *Romans* in *Britain*.
4. Of the *PICTS*.
5. Of the *SCOTS* ; and what way *FERGUS* came to be placed on the Throne.
6. *An Abridgement* of the *Lives* and *Reigns* of the *Kings* of *SCOTLAND*, from *Fergus* I. the Founder of the *Scots Monarchie*, to King *James* VI. his Acceffion to the Crown of *England* ; Together with fome of their *Contemporaries*, and feveral remarkable Actions, which happned in other Nations, during the Reign of thefe Kings, and of the *Divifes* of the Royal Family of STUARTS.

    In thefe Chapters, it is to be found, what is material and remarkable in Fordon, Boetius, Leflie, Buchanan, *and other Scots* Hiftorians: *And likewife feveral other remarkable Paffages, which hath not been hitherto publifhed, by any Writer of the Hiftory of* SCOTLAND.

7. Of the Antiquity of the *ROYAL LINE*.

    This Chapter is an Abreviat of the Debate, betwixt Sir George Mackenzie, *and the Bifhop of St.* Afaph, *and Doctor* Stillingfleet: *wherein all the ftrongeft Arguments adduced againft this Antiquity, and the Anfwers thereto are ranked together, one by one.*

8 Of

One of Slezer's many petitions to Parliament.

The ANCIENT AND PRESENT STATE OF SCOTLAND

After the publication of the *Theatrum Scotiae*, Slezer continued to work on his survey of the nation, which was to be completed with the publication of a work entitled 'The Ancient and Present State of Scotland'. This was to consist of material which he had held back from the *Theatrum Scotiae* – mainly the prospects of private houses – together with new material describing the offices of state, and prospects and groundplans of the royal palaces and castles. The proposed text of the first part of this book, consisting of eight chapters, survives. The text is entitled 'Of Ancient Scotland, and its Ancient People',[17] and, as with the text of the *Theatrum Scotiae*, each page is signed by both Slezer and Sibbald. However, this text was not used directly by Slezer to form the first chapters of his 'The Ancient and Present State of Scotland'. Slezer petitioned the Scots Parliament for assistance in order to publish this new work, and the Committee for Trade was asked to examine his project. Slezer was more than successful in his submission before this Committee, as not only did they recommend that the 'Ancient and Present State of Scotland' should be paid for out of general taxation, but that Slezer should be reimbursed for his expenditure on the *Theatrum Scotiae* from the same source. Parliament, however, while accepting most of the recommendations of the Committee, disregarded their views as to the method of payment, and simply added Slezer's name to the beneficiaries of the 1695 Tunnage Act. Amongst the others who shared the proceeds of this tax on shipping landing goods at Scots ports was another former collaborator of Sir Robert Sibbald, John Adair, who was producing a sea atlas of Scottish waters. The collection of this tax was both erratic and inefficient, with the result that Slezer received very little from it.

Slezer had completed the compilation of 'The Ancient and Present State of Scotland' and was only awaiting the finance to bring it to publication, as the high costs of engraving the drawings and plans combined with Slezer's own deteriorating financial position meant that he could not contemplate publishing the volumes on his own. In a number of printed schedules Slezer made a case for the publication of 'The Ancient and Present State of

Scotland' by giving a detailed description of the proposed format and contents of the two volumes, and although there was some slight variation in these documents, they all give a good impression of what the completed project would have been like. The following schedule is an example of one of the most detailed of these documents.[18]

REPRESENTATION. For Captain JOHN SLEZER, Annent the History, and Present State of Scotland to be published by him.

The Captain, since, and upon the Faith of, the Act of Tunnage, has so far advanced his Work, that the Lords of His Majesties Privy Council has appointed a Committee of their own Number, to revise it: And hoping, the Work will give Satisfaction, both in the Description & Draughts, to all, who are Lovers of their Countrey, and of what is Curious and Diverting, he humbly offers an View of the Work it self, and of the Contents of it, to His Majesties High Comissioner, and the Right Honourable the Estates of Parliament.

The Work is to be Printed upon Paper of the same Size and Fynness, with the Title Page; and the FIRST VOLUME consists of Two Parts: In the First of which, are these following Chapters.

1   Of BRITTAIN in general.

2   Of SCOTLAND in general.

3   Of the WALLS built by the Romans in Britain.

4   Of the Picts.

5   Of the SCOTS; and what way Fergus came to be placed on the throne.

6   An abridgement of the Lives and Reigns of the Kings of SCOTLAND, from Fergus I. the Founder of the Scots Monarchie, to King James VI. his Accession to the Crown of England; Together with some of their Contemporaries, and several remarkable Actions, which happned in other Nations, during the Reign of these Kings, and of the Divises of the Royal Family of STUARTS.

In these Chapters, it is to be found, what is material and remarkable in Fordon, Boetius, Leslie, Buchanan, and other Scots Historians: And likewise several other remarkable Passages, which hath not been hitherto published, by any Writer of the History of SCOTLAND.

7   Of the Antiquity of the ROYAL LINE.

   This Chapter is an Abreviat of the Debate, betwixt Sir George Mackenzie, and the Bishop of St Asaph, and Doctor Stillingfleet: wherein all the strongest Arguments adduced against this Antiquity, and the Answers thereto are ranked together, one by one.

8   Of the Mistake and Partiality of those, who pretend, that the Crown of SCOTLAND was ever Feudatory to the Crown of England; And that the Kings of SCOTLAND payed Homage to these of England, upon that account.

   Herein is breifly to be had, what, with very great Learning and Judgement, hath been writ on this Subject by Sir Thomas Craig, and Sir George Mackenzie, and likewise Answers to Mr Tyrrel's Insinuations of this Homage, in the first Volume of his History of England.

9   Of the Marriage of King Robert II. King of SCOTLAND, containing a Vindication of King Robert III. his Son, from the Imputation of Bastardy.

   This Chapter contains the summ of what hath been published, to great Advantage, by my Lord Viscount of Tarbat, upon this Subject; And likeways some other Documents, relating to this Affair, found in the Scots Colledge at Paris, and published since his Lordships Vindication: with a Confutation of Mr. Jones: who, in his Tragical History of the Stuarts, treats the Royal Family, with very much Indiscretion, on the account of this Fictitious Bastardy of Robert III. and endeavours to redargue my Lord Tarbat's Proofs, of the Legitimacie of that Prince.

10   Of the Precedencie due to Kings of SCOTLAND.

The Second PART. is composed of these Chapters

1   Of the PARLIAMENT; of the Members thereof; Of the way of calling of the Parliament; and Electing Commissioners for Shires and Burghs-Royal; The way of Rideing of the Parliament, and of the Power and Procedure in Parliament.

2   Of the CONVENTION of ESTATES,

3   Of the PRIVY-COUNCIL and of OFFICERS of STATE.

4   Of the THESAURIE and EXCHEQUER.

5 Of the SESSION and COLLEDGE of JUSTICE, and Institution thereof, Of the Ordinary and Extraordinary SENATORS, Of the ADVOCATS, CLERKS and WRITTERS; Of the OUTER and INNER-HOUSE, and the manner of Proceeding therein.

6 Of the Justiciary-Court, commonly called the Criminal-Court; As also, of the Justice-General, Commissioners of Justiciary and Assizes.

7 Of the High-Court of ADMIRALITY.

8 Of the HIGH-CONSTABIE; or the Earl of Eroll's Court.

9 Of the Commissary-Court.

10 Of Inferior-Courts; such as Sheriff-Courts, Courts of Regality, Stewartrie, Baillie and Burrough-Courts, and Justices of Peace.
  The Description, of Judicatories, in these Chapters, is more full than any hitherto published.

VOLUME II. Contains these several CHAPTERS.

1 Of the NOBILITY of SCOTLAND.
  Herein, after a short Introduction, annent Nobility in general, is to be found the Number and Titles of our present Noblemen; with their Sirnames, and Titles of their Eldest Sons.

2 Contains the Coats of Arms of the Nobility; with their Supporters; Crests, and Motto's all curiously drawn; Together with the Blazoning, of each Atchievment, placed under it.

3 Of the Precedencie observed, amongst the Subjects of SCOTLAND, where unto is added, a list of the Knight Barronets, in this Kingdom.

4 The Form of Creation and Investiture of a Nobleman in SCOTLAND.

5 Of the Constitution of the Herauld-Office, and of the Lyon King at ARMS; The Order, observed at his Coronation; The Way of Reversing of Arms, after Sentence of Forfaulture; And the Way and Manner of Publishing the KING'S Proclamations.

6 Of the Military and Equestrial Order of St Andrew, commonly called the Order of Scotland, or of the THISTLE; containing an account of the Institution and Solemnity, observed at the Investiture of the Knight

of that Order, with curious draughts of their Badges. Whereunto is added, a breif Discription of the other Orders of Knight-hood in Europe, and when Instituted, with Draughts of their respective Marks of Honour. From which the Antiquity of the Order of Scotland does more plainly appear.

7   Of the Solemnities, which have been observed, in Scotland, on Occasion of Baptisms and Funerals; The first illustrated by these observed, at the Baptism of Prince Henry, Son to King James VI. And the second, by the Funeral Solemnities, of the Duke of Rothes Lord High Chancellar of Scotland; Represented in a most curious and exact Draught, upon four sheets of Royal Paper.

8   The Cavalcade, or Solemnity, observed at the first Session of Parliament; as it was last performed, in the year 1685. (Since which time there has been no such Solemnitie) most neatly drawn, on three Sheets of Royal Paper.

These things are so Curious, and the Draughts so neat, that, it is hoped, they will recommend themselves, to any, who views them,

9   The Prospects of His Majesties Castles and Palaces; With the Prospects of several Houses, belonging to Noblemen and Gentlemen; and a short Discription of them.

These Prospects are very fine and curious; some are already engraven; others are drawn; and some are drawing: With the Plans of their Stories and ground Plat of the Gardens. And the number of these will be, according to the Encouragement the Captain recieves seing they cannot be drawn and engraven, without great Expences.

10   The prospect of several Cities, Royal-Burghs, Universities, Towns and Hospitals, within this Kingdom; with a short Discription of each place: whereunto is added, an account of the Trade and Manufactories in the Kingdom.

11   Monasticon Scotiae; containing a short account of the Monasteries, and other Religious Houses, and the several Orders of Friars, Monks and Nuns, which were in Scotland, before the Reformation; with the Sculptures of some of these Buildings.

Though these Monasteries were Nests of Luxurie; yet the Magnificence of the Buildings, does contribute to the Honour of the Nation.

This whole Work, being composed of Variety of Matter, so agreeable to all Gentlemen, and of Draughts, so pleasant and curious, it is hoped, it will meet with Acceptance and Encouragement.

Another version is slightly more solicitous of additional material.

> *The Second Part of this Volume Contains the following Chapters.*
> *I. The Prospects of His Majesties Castles and Palaces, and those of several houses belonging to Noblemen, Gentlemen: Together with the plans of the respective stories and appartments; and the ground-plats of the garden and avenues belonging to the above-mentioned houses. As also a short description of each house; and if the proprietors of them, upon due advertisment given them, are pleased to give unto the author a short account of their Families, it shall be likewise inserted.*[19]

One of the sections of the text which Slezer mentions in his submission, that bearing on the office of the Lord Lyon and its workings, survives in manuscript in the National Library of Scotland.[20] It is clear from the way that this document has been altered that it was originally a reply to specific enquiries by Slezer about the work of the Lord Lyon and his court. Slezer has taken this letter, and, by removing the evidence of its status as a reply and adding only a few sentences, has converted it directly into part of the text of 'The Ancient and Present State of Scotland', where it forms the bulk of chapter 5 of volume II. This is an interesting survival of one of Slezer's sources and might have been considered only a time-saving or cost-cutting exercise in the rush to produce a substantial text to set before the Estates of Parliament. But an accusation which John Adair was to bring against him in 1701 throws more light on the question. Since Slezer and Adair were both beneficiaries of the Tunnage Act, and rivals for the same resources, it was perhaps inevitable that they should quarrel. Adair says of Slezer:

> *But it ought to be considered that the Parliament, at that tyme, did not know that the Capt. wanted qualifications to performe what he undertook; for all men of knowledge are convinced that the wrytting of the Ancient and Present State of Scotland trwely is a sufficient task for four or five of the most learned and experienced men in the Kingdom, and these well seen in the historie, geographie, the lawes and constitutions, the antiquitys and naturall history of the Nation, al which the Captain ane illiterat stranger, can not pretend to understand; only, to amaze the Countrey, he hath gathered together a big volume of scraps, from many different hands, most of them as unlearned as himself, so that its thought strange how such a designe is not only allowed but incouraged.*[21]

Slezer rebuts Adair's accusation that he is an illiterate foreigner, who is only regurgitating other scholars' work, in yet another petition to the Scots Parliament which he wrote from the sanctuary of Holyrood around 1705.

But an Undertaking of this Nature seeming at first view something out of the Road of a Forreigner, and one of a military Profession, it has made a very disadvantageous impression in severals, in so far that some have condemned it, who never had opportunity to peruse one Sheet of the said Work. Your Petitioner therefore does in all humility offer to be considered, that he can scarcely be look't upon any longer as a Stranger, having had the Honour to be settled in this Nation upwards of Thirty Years, during which time he had leasure, and sufficient Encouragement to inform himself of every thing that could contribute to make this Work acceptable, neither has he spared Pains nor Charges to Consult and seek Assistance from such persons, on whose Advice and Opinion he could intirely rely for the exactness of what he undertook to publish.[22]

In fact the cut-and-paste methods which Slezer employed were not unusual for his time, and even fifty years later Maitland, in his history of Edinburgh, made up the text in large part from earlier sources, including the *Theatrum Scotiae*.

Visual Material for 'The Ancient and Present State of Scotland'

Slezer's plans for 'The Ancient and Present State of Scotland' were laid on a grand scale. In one of the petitions of 1695 he indicates that there are still one hundred engravings to be made for the project and the same number of pages of text. Only the best materials would be used – paper at 40 shillings a ream, a cost of 20 shillings per book for the paper alone.

Slezer by this stage planned to re-use most of the plates engraved for the *Theatrum Scotiae* within the two-volume 'Ancient and Present State of Scotland'. A few (seven or eight) would be removed: these he describes as 'being the prospects of little mean things, or else they are not weel done at all'.[23]

Only a small portion of the new visual material gathered for 'The Ancient and Present State of Scotland' was engraved in Slezer's lifetime, including the plates of private houses which were held back from the *Theatrum Scotiae*. He lists all the engraved but unpublished plates in one of his submissions to the Scots Parliament. These are, 'The King's Statue [Charles II] in the Parliament Closs'; 'the Toun of Ed'r in tuo great sheets'; 'Herriot's Hospitall, twice drawn'; 'Three Plates of Lauder and a title plate for the same'; 'Castle of Ed'r'; 'Dalkeith'; 'Castle of Gordon'; 'Culross'; 'Glams, with the ground stories'; 'The Weems'; 'The prospects of Hatton, and tuo plates of the ground draughts'.[24]

The double plate of Edinburgh (SL.58), entitled 'The Prospect of Edinburgh from Ye North' in its published form, is mentioned in Slezer's list of charges as:

For drawing and ingraving the toun of Edr in tuo great sheets,
£20:00:00

The prospect was taken from a point now located just to the east of the Nelson Monument on Calton Hill, from which a number of depicted buildings can still be seen today. This double plate appears only in the 1718 editions of the *Theatrum Scotiae*, and a new dedication to the Marquess

of Annandale was engraved along the bottom of both plates shortly before publication. This prospect was originally engraved as two separate sheets, as the awkward way in which the two sheets join attests, but one impression of the right plate survives in its original form. This impression,[25] bound in a copy of the 1719 edition, is titled in both Latin and English ('Prospectus Civitatis Edinburgenae. The Prospect of Edinburgh from Ye North'), in a similar way to the plates of the *Theatrum Scotiae*. The left plate shows the Canongate and Holyroodhouse, so may have been titled differently. In Smith's 1728-9 edition an enlarged version of this plate was published.

The Prospect of Edinburgh from ye North. (SL.58)

All three plates of Lauder (Thirlestane), Edinburgh and its Castle, Glamis, and Culross House, were all titled correctly, but some of the plates which were published in later editions were not.

The three plates of Thirlestane Castle at Lauder which John, Duke of Lauderdale had financed in the 1670s were eventually published in 1718 and 1719. Lauderdale had been the virtual ruler of Scotland for Charles II

John, Duke of Lauderdale, engraving by Goldar. Author's Collection.

The Ground Story of Thirlestane Castle. The First Story of Thirlestane Castle. (SL.63)

Lauder Castle. (SL.61)

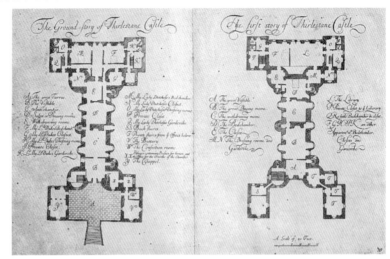

Thirlestane Castle. (SL.62)

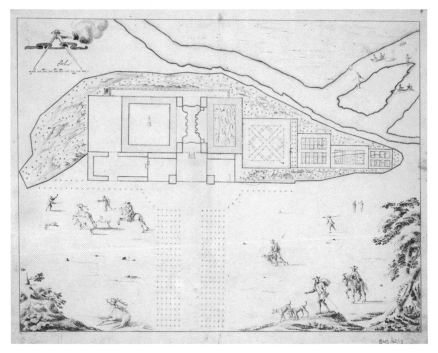

Slezer's plan of Thirlestane estate. Copyright: Royal Commission on the Ancient and Historical Monuments of Scotland.

and during his years of power refurbished and remodelled many family properties. He employed a cousin of his second wife, Sir William Bruce, who was Scotland's leading architect, to design these improvements.

Hatton House, the home of Lauderdale's brother (and his successor as 3rd Earl) was also engraved, and appeared mistitled 'Argile-House'(SL.67) in the 1719 edition of the *Theatrum Scotiae*. The House was damaged by fire in 1952 and completely demolished three years later.

Hatton House ('Argile-House').
(SL.67)

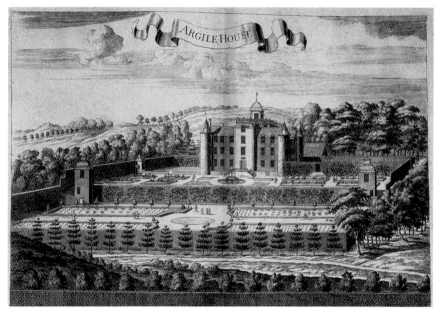

The enormous engraving of Heriot's Hospital was mis-titled 'Boghen-gieght' in mistake for the Duke of Gordon's castle. This engraving of Heriot's Hospital is the largest of the published plates, made on a copper plate measuring 420 × 540mm. None of the surviving prospect drawings is conceived on this sort of scale, though the Holyrood drawings are certainly larger than most of those published in the *Theatrum Scotiae*. What may have been destined for reproduction on plates of this size were the plans of fortifications and the royal palaces which Slezer had prepared and which are mentioned in his proposals.

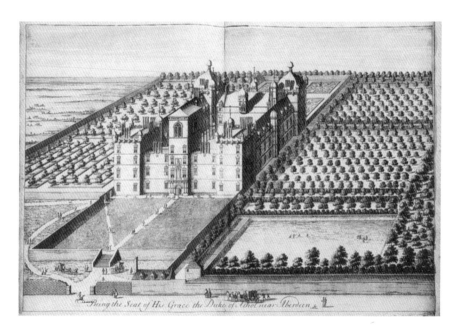

Heriot's Hospital ('Boghengieght').
(SL.66)

The plate itself went through a number of changes. It originally had a ribbon title 'Boghengieght', referring to the castle of the Duke of Gordon. Sometime after the death of White in 1703 and before 1715 the plate came into the possession of J. Nutting, who added 'Sold by J Nutting Engraver & Print Seller at Ye Gold & Blew-Fanns in Fleet Street near Salisbury Court' to the plate. The print bound in the National Library of Scotland's 1719 edition has had this addition removed along with the title, and 'Being the seat of his Grace the Duke of Athol near Aberdeen' has been added. (Atholl House can be seen in the Dunkeld plate, SL.24.) Unfortunately, the impression bound in with the British Library's copy of the 1728-9 edition is in the earlier state! The matter was further complicated by Dr Jamieson who had a new engraving of this prospect made for the 1814 edition. For this, the copper plate from an old map was re-used, and evidence of its earlier use can still seen on clear impressions. Jamieson used a '1719' impression to make this new plate, but corrected the 'Athol' to 'Gordon', and added the title 'Bogen=Gight'. The 1874 facsimile reproduces the 1719 image with the original ribbon title transferred to the field on the left of the buildings. As this plate was only published in two editions (and the 1719 edition is extremely rare), this prospect is one of the rarest as well as the most complex of the Slezer prints.

The plate depicting the Castle of Wemyss (SL.68) was issued with the title 'Donotter Castle'. The plate titled 'Glamms House'(SL.64), which during the nineteenth century had been claimed as an early view of Glamis, taken before Earl Patrick's improvements, was, however, clearly at odds with a contemporary view of the Castle in the background of a painting of Earl Patrick and his children. As there is an extant drawing, identical in all details to this prospect and entitled 'Dalkeith Castle',[26] there can be little doubt that Dalkeith is the correct location for this prospect.

Left: *Wemyss Castle ('Donotter Castle'). (SL.68)*
Right: *Dalkeith Castle ('Glamms House'). (SL.64)*

Castle Gordon ('The Castle of Inverero'). (SL.65)

The remaining plate, 'The Castle of Inverero'(SL.65), depicts Castle Gordon. Pennant on his tour of the Highlands in the eighteenth century was told by members of the Gordon family that this plate depicted Castle Gordon, and this is almost certainly correct; but, as with Dalkeith, massive rebuilding during the eighteenth century changed the old castle beyond recognition, so it cannot be proved conclusively. No impressions of the Lauder title plate, the groundplans of Hatton and Glamis, or that of the statue of Charles II can be traced. In one of Slezer's later submissions he gives a slightly different list of the engraved plates, adding Dunottar Castle and the House of Dunkeld. This statement may have been either the cause, or the result, of the mistitling of two of the plates – Dunottar for Wemyss, and the Heriot's Hospital plate with 'Being the seat of His Grace the Duke of Athol near Aberdeen'.

Patrick, Earl of Strathmore, engraving by R. White. Author's Collection.

The real plate of Glamis was never used in any edition of the *Theatrum Scotiae*, although the plate of Dalkeith, mistitled 'Glamms House', was printed in the 1719 and later editions. The original copper plate (the only Slezer copper plate to survive) was rediscovered at Glamis in the 1970s. The plate is signed and dated by Robert White and the titling contains an elaborate explanation of the royal and ancient line of the Earl's family. White also engraved a portrait of Earl Patrick, also dated 1686, when the Earl was a member of the Privy Council of James VII. There is no indication in any of Slezer's proposals that portraits would be included anywhere within 'The Ancient and Present State of Scotland'.

Top: *The frontis=piece of the Castle of Glammiss. (SL.73) Copyright: Royal Commission on the Ancient and Historical Monuments of Scotland.*
Above: *Glamis today.*
Left: *Copper plate of Glamis engraved by Robert White. By permission of Strathmore Estates.*

One final plate (SL.72) exists which may have a connection with the *Theatrum Scotiae*. This plate appears only in the final volume of Joseph Smith's *Nouveau Theatre de la Grande Bretagne*, published in 1729. This volume consists of about half of the plates from the *Theatrum Scotiae*, the rest being plates by Kip after Knyff from the *Britannia Illustrata*, which was published in 1707 and depicts perspectives of gentlemen's houses. This plate is of a similar size and format to the Slezer plates. The plate is engraved in a style close to that of the double plate of Edinburgh (SL.58), and shows

The 'Estampe Emblematique'.
Author's Collection. (SL.72)

a stately house in the middle distance of the right side of the plate and a small town in the farther distance on the left. The plate has had the centre foreground re-engraved to make a political print out of a landscape. It is untitled, but described on the contents page as:

> *Estampe Emblematique sur la mort de Charles I. decapite le 30 Janvier 1648/49, & sur les trois Princesses fils, qui etoient alors fugatifs.*

The additions to the plate have been copied from an earlier engraving.[27] The broken crown and sceptre with the tree cut down clearly represent the death of Charles I. The crown which decorates the tallest of the scion branches represents Charles II, but though the iconography is clear the political significance is out of date. During the Commonwealth, the ownership of such an image would have been dangerous; after the restoration of Charles II it might still have had some currency; but after Charles II's death in 1685 the iconography would have been redundant; and a Jacobite reworking of the plate would have crowned the second branch.

It will probably never be known for certain who made this plate or why it was changed in such a strange way, or whether indeed it has any connection with 'The Ancient and Present State of Scotland' other than having been published with the other Slezer plates in 1729. It is, however, possible that Robert White or one of his successors was attempting to make use of a decorative plate for which they were never likely to be paid. As to its location, the most probable site is Scone. If this is the location, the later additions have some relevance as it was at Scone that Kings of Scotland were crowned in ancient times, and where Charles II was crowned King in 1651.

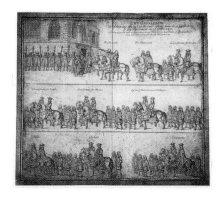

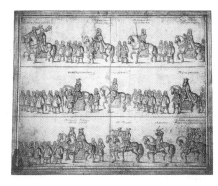

In Slezer's schedule for 'The Ancient and Present State of Scotland', two drawings of processions are mentioned prominently. 'The Funeral Solemnities of the Duke of Rothes, on three sheets of Royal Paper' (the same size as the paper of the *Theatrum Scotiae*), and 'The Riding of Parliament', taken at the Parliament of 1685. Both these sets of drawings were bought in the eighteenth century by Thomas Sommers, who gave them to the Advocates' Library in Edinburgh in 1803. The drawings of the Riding to Parliament were later engraved, and both sets of drawings are now held in the National Library of Scotland.[28]

Drawing of the Cavalcade or Riding of Parliament.

Slezer also lists drawings of the Palace of Holyroodhouse. One such drawing was later engraved for publication in Maitland's history of Edinburgh. This view is described by Slezer as 'tuice drawen', and two drawings of this prospect survive, one in the National Galleries of Scotland,[29] and one in the print room of the British Museum.[30] This second drawing is attributed only to the workshop of Sir William Bruce (the architect of the refurbished Holyrood), but the perspective of these views has much in common with the published prospects of Heriot's Hospital and the University of Glasgow.

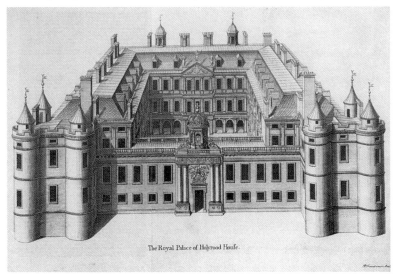

The Royal Palace of Holyrood House.

Holyroodhouse, from William Maitland, History of Edinburgh, *(Edinburgh, 1753).*

Another Holyrood view finds its way into William Adam's *Vitruvius Scoticus*: an engraving by Mazel after Wyck which shows the interior of the Chapel Royal as it appeared in 1688. At this date, the remains of the Abbey Church were fitted out as the Chapel of the Order of the Thistle, with the throne and stalls for the individual knights. The scale of this engraving

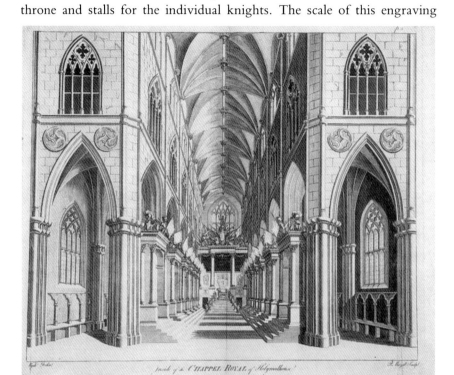

'Inside of the Chappel Royal of Holyroodhouse', engraving by Mazel. Author's Collection.

is consistent with its original having been designed for 'The Ancient and Present State of Scotland'. Slezer's description of this particular drawing in the printed schedule is uncharacteristically specific:

> *The perspective of the insyde of the Abbay Church, with the stalls of the Knights of the Thistle, tuice drawn, once in Scotland, and the other by Mr Whyte at London.*[31]

The size of the engraving would probably equal the dimensions of the drawing and gives a good idea of the grand scale in which Slezer conceived this project. These two depictions are of a much higher quality than most of his other prospects. They are both perspective views, strictly symmetrical, and for this reason may not be the work of Slezer. Wyck's landscapes as seen in Blome's *The Gentlemans Recreation* are rather different. It is possible that these perspective prospects may be the work of Loggan's collaborator Kickius, as noted by Vertue, but Kickius had returned to London by 1688, the year in which this drawing must have been made.

Sir William Bruce (*c.*1630-1710) was Scotland's leading architect during the later Stuart period, and a number of the private houses which are

Sir William Bruce, by John Michael Wright. Scottish National Portrait Gallery.

mentioned by Slezer in his schedule for 'The Ancient and Present State of Scotland' were designed by him. Two, Kinross and Balcaskie, had been built as his own homes, and Bruce was also employed by Lauderdale to work on both Thirlestane and Brunstane. A full description of the Kinross entry is given in one of Slezer's many petitions for 'The Ancient and Present State of Scotland':

> *The house of Kinross in perspective, all the different stories of it, together with the general ground-plot of the said house, representing the garden, office-houses, and other conveniences of it.*[32]

This description matches a pair of surviving drawings of the house and grounds which have been attributed to Sir William Bruce. These drawings are very similar to the set of drawings (attributed to Slezer) which represent the gardens and fabric of Thirlestane Castle. Whether they are all by Bruce, or all by Slezer, or even a collaboration between the two, they certainly represent the material which was intended for the Kinross entry in 'The Ancient and Present State of Scotland'. It is also possible that all these related drawings could be by Alexander Edward who made many plans of houses and gardens at this time. The plans also give some idea of the splendour and usefulness of the project had it only been completed. One possible reason for Slezer keeping quiet about any collaboration with Bruce (apart from his habitual reticence regarding sources) was the latter's resignation from all his public appointments after the Revolution of 1688. Suspected of Jacobite sympathies, he was on two occasions imprisoned in Edinburgh Castle.

Drawings of Kinross House and gardens. Copyright: Royal Commission on the Ancient and Historical Monuments of Scotland.

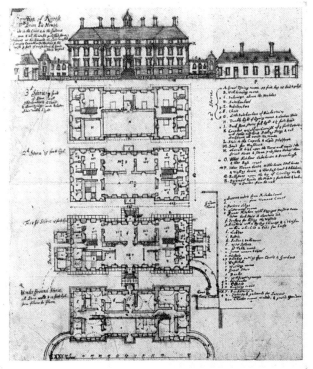 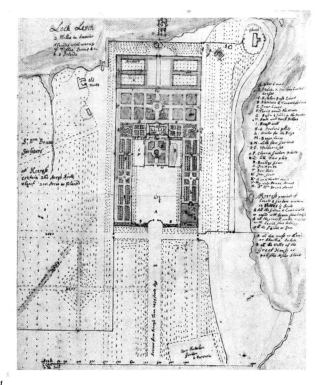

*Drawing of 'Burnt Island,
Enchkieth'. National Gallery
of Scotland.*

The SLEZER DRAWINGS

There are a number of drawings held in both public and private collections which are connected either directly or indirectly with the *Theatrum Scotiae* or Slezer's other projects. Many of these drawings, especially those now in the collection of Edinburgh City Libraries, are delicately drawn and fully finished in Indian Ink washes. The copperplate titles and heavy line borders indicate that these prospects were ready to send directly to the engravers, but they differ greatly in both size and shape from the standard dimensions and format of the engravings in the *Theatrum Scotiae*. It is unlikely that Slezer would have scaled down his ideas for this second volume, indeed, surviving plates indicate the reverse. These drawings do seem to be constructed to a set format, and it is likely that they indicate his original ideas regarding the size and shape of the engravings.

A considerable number of these drawings by Slezer have survived. The majority are of places of military or strategic significance. Castles such as Edinburgh and Stirling predominate, but drawings of ports such as Burntisland and Leith, which do not feature in the *Theatrum Scotiae*, are particularly interesting.

The drawing of 'Burnt Island and Enchkeith' shows a wide prospect of the north coast of the Firth of Forth with Burntisland on the left. To the right, it looks out to the mouth of the Forth with the Bass Rock and North Berwick Law in the far distance. The waves and the boat added to the foreground have the unfortunate effect of making the substantial island of Inchkeith seem little bigger than a rock. The closer view of 'Burnt Island' shows the defences of the harbour as well as a closer view of the town's square-built post-reformation church.

Leith, as the port of Edinburgh, has always played an important part in Scotland's history. Three of Slezer's views of Leith show the town from a distance. One, the prospect of 'Edenborrow and Lieth from the Island Enchkeith', shows the relationship between the city and the port at this date, and the look of the landscape before the enclosure of much of the surrounding countryside. The second is a slightly nearer view, from the east end of Leith Links; and the third is a prospect of Leith from the south,

Drawing of 'Burnt Island'. National Gallery of Scotland.

'Edenborrow and Lieth from the Island Enchkieth'. Edinburgh City Libraries.

Top left: *'The Prospect of Edenborrow and Lieth from the links of Lieth.' Edinburgh City Libraries.*
Top right: *'The Piere of Lieth.' Edinburgh City Libraries.*
Above: *'The Prospect of Lieth from Leith-wind at Edenborrow.' Edinburgh City Libraries.*

viewed from Leith Wynd in Edinburgh. The final prospect of Leith is a close-up view of the wooden pier of the harbour, taken from the shore just to the east of the town.

A larger number of drawings of Stirling survive than of any other Scottish town, with the exception of Edinburgh. This is not really surprising, as Stirling was not only a military centre, second only in importance to the capital, but the site of an important royal palace. In addition to the three

Top left: *Drawing of 'Sterling from the Abby Cragg'. National Gallery of Scotland.*
Top right: *Drawing of 'Sterling from the side of the Toarre Wood'. National Gallery of Scotland.*
Bottom left: *Drawing of 'No. 1, plan of Stirling castle'. Public Record Office, MPF 246.*
Bottom right: *Drawing of 'No. 2, Sterling Castle from the North'. Public Record Office, MPF 246.*

plates from the *Theatrum Scotiae*, these drawings give a unique picture of the town in the seventeenth century, before the Castle had lost its mediaeval gatehouse. Slezer also produced a detailed plan of the Castle, which would have formed a decorative plate in 'The Ancient and Present State of Scotland'.

Edinburgh, as capital of Scotland and the seat of government, might at first glance seem under-represented in Slezer's work. Only two prospects of Edinburgh were included in the first edition of the *Theatrum Scotiae*: a view of the Castle and town from the south, and a view from Dean Village. However, the early list of prospects indicates that a number of other plates of the city had been intended for the first edition, and the original Latin text of the book deals with the City of Edinburgh (and its neighbouring burghs of Portsburgh and Canongate) in some detail. This perhaps accounts for the large number of extant drawings of Edinburgh, which combine to provide an accurate record of the city in the late seventeenth century. It might also be expected that at least some of these surviving drawings would have been used to make up Edinburgh prospects for 'The Ancient and Present State of Scotland' had this project ever been published.

Slezer made his series of prospects from vantage points in a circle round the City. Two of the drawn prospects which have not survived are unfortunately those taken from the high point on Calton Hill; these were used to engrave the double prospect of Edinburgh from the north (SL.58) which was only published after Slezer's death. It is possible that these drawings were separated from the others simply because they were needed by the printmakers.

The Edinburgh drawings focus mainly on the west end of the city around the Castle and the east end of the Canongate around the Palace of Holyroodhouse. The studies include one drawing of the front of the Castle taken from the top of the High Street, and an internal view of some of the defences within the Castle walls. This latter view shows the great gun 'Mons Meg' lying abandoned. As the drawing is undated, it is not certain whether it was made before or after the gun was last fired. Mons Meg was charged to celebrate the birthday of the Duke of York in 1680, but, instead

'The Entry of the Castle of Edenburgh as it was in the year 1675.' Edinburgh City Libraries.

'The New Retrenchment within the Castle of Edenborrow.' Edinburgh City Libraries.

of firing its massive stone missile, it exploded. Slezer might well have been a witness to this near disaster, but it was probably the Master Gunner of Edinburgh Castle, rather than Slezer or any of the Artillery Train, who was responsible. It is typical of Slezer's drawings that the figures in this prospect give a very distorted idea of the size of the gun they seem to be guarding: even Mons Meg is not as big as it appears from the drawing.

The two views from the north show little of the buildings within the Castle, which are mainly situated on the east, but the view of the 'North Side of the Castle' gives a good view of the Church of St Cuthbert at the west end of the North Loch. The rebuilt Church still stands at the west end of Princes Street gardens. The prospect taken from 'The North Loch' was made from a point which is now situated at the west end of Princes Street, and shows the town from an unusual angle. The Castle naturally dominates, and the position of the High Street can be deduced from the position of the crown of St Giles, and the spires of the Tron and the Netherbow Port. From this prospect it is much easier to see the higher ground which the old city walls followed and which was guarded by the Netherbow Port which contains the City of Edinburgh, and below which

Below: *'The North side of the Castle of Edenborrow.'* Edinburgh City Libraries.
Bottom: *'The Prospect of the Castle and Citty of Edenborrow from the North Loch'.* Edinburgh City Libraries.

the burgh of the Canongate was situated. The Chapel of Holyrood can just be seen in the far distance, half hidden by the Collegiate Church of the Holy Trinity. This church was situated just outside the city walls, beyond the North Port where the wester road to Leith entered the city. Though it was never completed, the Trinity Church was one of Edinburgh's finest historic buildings. It was dismantled to make way for the railway station in the nineteenth century.

The drawings from the south give more detail of both the buildings within the Castle and in the city. 'The Prospect of Edinburgh from Henry's Work' (Heriot's) shows the west wall of the city's defences which surround Heriot's Hospital, dip towards the Grassmarket where the West Port gave access to the independent burgh of Portsburgh, and rise to join the fortifications of the Castle. From this vantage point little can be seen of Portsburgh or the Grassmarket, but to the right of St Giles stands the Parliament House which dominates the southern slope of the hill. To the right of this, at the head of the Grassmarket, is the tower of the Chapel of St Mary Magdalene, which still stands today, but, like the Parliament House, is dwarfed and hidden by subsequent development. Heriot's Hospital stands

'The Prospect of Edinborow from Henrys Worke.' Edinburgh City Libraries.

'The South side of the Castle of Edinborrow.' Edinburgh City Libraries.

on the hill on the extreme right, and the square tower just behind it is that of the Greyfriars Church. This drawing is almost identical to the 'Prospect of Edinburgh Castle from the South' (SL.1). Slezer made another drawing of the city from the same angle, but from a greater distance. This shows the full extent of the Castle and Arthur's Seat. A rather closer view of the south side of the Castle, taken from the grounds of Heriot's Hospital, shows the whole length of the defensive wall stretching down from the Castle to the West Port.

One of Slezer's drawings of Edinburgh from the east end, 'The Prospect of Edinborrow from St Anthony's Well', was viewed from St Anthony's Chapel in the Queen's Park. This vantage point was to become a favourite spot for artists in the late eighteenth and nineteenth centuries, but Slezer's view is the first. All the main features of the City of Edinburgh and the burgh of the Canongate are shown in this prospect. The Chapel Royal and the Palace of Holyroodhouse are at the right, with Calton Hill behind them; moving up the High Street the first small spire is that of the Canongate Tolbooth (where Slezer was imprisoned in 1689), followed by the tower of the Netherbow Port, the Tron Church, St Giles and the Castle. To the left of the Castle, the last building that can be seen on the horizon is the Chapel of St Mary Magdalene.

'The West side of the Castle and City of Edenburrow.' Edinburgh City Libraries.

'The Prospect of Edinborrow from St. Anthony's Well.' Edinburgh City Libraries.

Restalrig (called 'Listerreck' by Slezer) was an important military base in the seventeenth century, and 'The Prospect of Edenborrow from Listerreck' shows a good view of the back of the Chapel Royal. A similar viewpoint, but within the Queen's Park, was used for 'The Prospect of Edinborrow Comeing from Musselborrow', which was taken from the east end of the Park, almost in direct line with the High Street. St Giles, the Tron and the Netherbow Port are crowded together by this particular viewpoint and it shows clearly that the larger area of the city was to the south of the High Street. Again the tower of St Mary Magdalene is prominent, but the Parliament House is not clear enough to be made a feature from this angle.

'The Prospect of Edenborrow from the Quarry Holes towards Leith' is another interesting drawing. The Quarry holes of the title were situated on the lowest eastern slopes of Calton Hill, near one of the two roads to Leith – the easter road (the wester being a continuation of Leith Wynd) – and Slezer's viewpoint is now called Abbeymount. The centre of the drawing follows the main east road towards the Watergate, the eastern entrance to the Canongate along the walls of the privy gardens of the Palace. The small building at the far end of the wall is one of the old gatehouses of the original Abbey which survives to this day and which is commonly known as Queen Mary's Bath. The arch and enclosure opposite this building is the Horse Pond, and to the extreme left of the prospect is the Croft an Righ.

Top: 'The Prospect of Edenborrow from Listerreck.' Edinburgh City Libraries. Middle: 'The Prospect of Edinborrow Comeing from Musselborrow.' Edinburgh City Libraries. Bottom: 'The Prospect of Edenborrow from the Quarry holes towards Leith'. Edinburgh City Libraries.

Trinity College Church, engraving
by Parr after John Elphinstone.

SLEZER'S LEGACY

When Slezer died in 1717 he left behind him more than just the *Theatrum Scotiae* and the remnants of 'The Ancient and Present State of Scotland': he also left a tradition of military draughtsmanship. Theodore Dury, Slezer's assistant, and John Elphinstone, both of whom were Engineer in Scotland, made plans and drawings. Elphinstone even published a series of engravings of important buildings in Edinburgh.

In the 1740s, the military in Scotland also employed the Sandby brothers, two outstanding English artists, to make plans and drawings. Thomas was a noted topographer, and Paul was a fine artist and an innovative printmaker who in turn influenced a number of Scottish printmakers, including David Allan and John Clerk of Eldin. The Sandby brothers were also known to use the camera obscura in their topographical work, and a watercolour of Roslin Castle by Paul shows such a device in use.

Paul Sandby, Roslin Castle, showing a lady using a camera obscura (c. 1775). Yale Center for British Art, Paul Mellon Collection.

Slezer's legacy also included his images of Scotland, which were re-used and re-issued for over a hundred years. On the expiry of Slezer's royal licence in 1707, the Dutch publishing house of Van der Aa reproduced the majority of his prospects in a reduced format. These plates were published in four different books between 1707 and 1727. Slezer himself may not have made any useful profits from his plates, but after his death in 1717 other publishers certainly did. Only a year later, in 1718, Slezer's copper plates were used for new editions of the *Theatrum Scotiae*. The text was reduced and new dedications were added to the titling on the plates. In 1719 an edition was issued by Joseph Smith, who may have been the owner of the plates as early as 1715. Smith later allowed J. Groenowegen and N. Prevost to publish around half the plates in 1728, in a supplement to his own *Nouveau Theatre de la Grande Bretagne* (3 vols, 1724). This was itself a compilation of plates which had appeared in other volumes. At this stage Smith was advertising that if any gentleman wished to have his seat included this could be arranged for a fee of five guineas. Smith published the remaining Slezer plates in a fourth volume of the *Nouveau Theatre* in 1729. Sometime after Smith, the plates were owned by the London firm of Bowles and Carver.

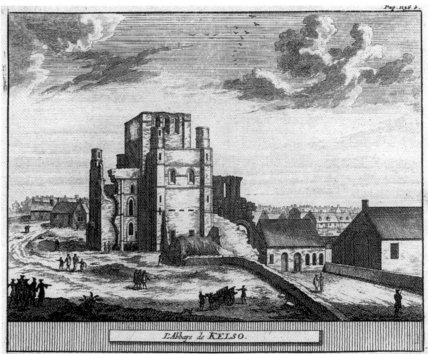

'L'Abbaye de Kelso', published by Van der Aa. Author's Collection.

The next full edition of the plates, published under the title *Views of the Principal Towns, Castles, Abbeys &c in Scotland*, was printed by Thomas Wilkinson of Cornhill in London in 1797, and although the plates were then over a hundred years old they were offered as contemporary views. In order to aid this deception, some of the more obviously seventeenth-century figures were removed and replaced by figures in contemporary dress. In addition to these 'period' figures, other additions were made: boats, fishermen, dogs, ducks, and, on the Aberdeen plate (SL.19), a decorative country cottage, completely out of scale. Some of the ancient buildings and ruins depicted were also dressed up with weeds to make them look more fashionably 'picturesque'.

The copper plates were rescued from obscurity by the Scottish antiquarian Dr Jamieson who had a limited edition of one hundred copies printed from them in 1814. He admits to the re-engraving of the missing plate of Heriot's Hospital for this edition, but remains silent about three other plates which were also re-engraved from earlier impressions. These were printed on different paper from the rest, watermarked 'J. Whatman 1810' and 'J. Whatman 1811'. It is not known what happened to the copper plates after Dr Jamieson had finished with them, but, as can be seen from the condition of most of the impressions of this final edition, they were in a poor state and no later impressions were made from them.

Some of the plates had impressions printed from them between editions, and a few collections may have been made up from these separate impressions (Smith's 1719 edition contains a number of plates bound up in this way). There is, however, in the National Library of Scotland, a collection of eight of the plates bound together with a title page, printed, according to this title page, in Edinburgh in 1692 and thus apparently predating the first edition of the *Theatrum Scotiae* by a year. But this book is simply a clever fake, made sometime before the 1718 edition by cleaning the plates to make them look newer than the first edition and removing the numbering. The copper plates had never been brought to Edinburgh. Slezer himself states that he had to go to London to oversee the publication of the book, and his engraver White was careful to hold the plates against full payment by Slezer, at one point threatening to sell them. The only copper plate to survive, that of Glamis, ended up in the possession of the Earl of Strathmore, who had, after all, paid for its manufacture.

Conclusion

Slezer's importance as a recorder of the State of Scotland, and as a gatherer of historical and visual material, can hardly be overestimated. Although much of Slezer's work was never published in his lifetime, other writers did make full use of his material after his death. The plans and drawings which survive give vital information to historians and archaeologists working today, as well as being delightful works of art in their own right. As an artist, his talents may have been modest, but he used his knowledge of science and art to record his adopted country as no-one had done before, preserving for ever a vision of Scotland as it was in his day.

A detail from the Kelso Abbey plate (SL.50) in the 1693 edition (top) and in the 1797 edition.

Title page of Eight Fine Views, *fraudulently dated 1692.*

Notes

A number of papers relating to John Slezer and John Adair are reprinted in *The Bannatyne Miscellany*, vol. II, edited by D. Laing (Edinburgh: The Bannatyne Club, 1827).

1. Slezer's petition of 1698. Laing VIII.
2. In 'To the reader' of the *Theatrum Scotiae* (1693).
3. Historical MSS Commission. Report X, para 1.
4. Glamis Book of Record of Patrick, Earl of Strathmore.
5. Slezer's petition of 1696. Laing III.
6. Ashmolean Museum Drawings Catalogue Vol. IV, Nos 234, 235, 236.
7. Slezer's 'Particular accompt of Debursements', 1696. Laing IV.
8. Slezer's 'Particular accompt of Debursements', 1696. Laing IV.
9. Walpole Society Vol. 18, 1930. Vertue MSS Vol. 1, p.105.
10. Slezer's 'Particular accompt of Debursements', 1696. Laing IV.
11. Slezer's 'Particular accompt of Debursements', 1696. Laing IV.
12. Slezer's Petition of 4 September 1696. Laing III.
13. Slezer's 'Particular accompt of Debursements', 1696. Laing IV.
14. National Library of Scotland, Adv MS 33.3.22.
15. Prospects and Antiquities of Scotland. National Library of Scotland, Adv MS 22.2.9, f.132.
16. National Library of Scotland, MS 22.2.9, f.132 v.
17. National Library of Scotland, MS 33.3.22.
18. Slezer's petition of 14 February 1698. Laing VI.
19. Slezer's printed prospectus of *c*.1698.
20. National Library of Scotland, Adv MS 29.3.4.
21. Answers for John Adair, Geographer, to the memorial given in by Capt. Slezer against him. 1701. (Produced before the Committee 29 July 1701.) Laing Adair XV.
22. The Representation of John Slezer. National Library of Scotland, APS. 4.83.52.
23. Slezer's petition of 1696. Laing III.
24. Slezer's 'Particular accompt of Debursements', 1696. Laing IV.
25. Untraced but reproduced in W.M. Parker, 'Scotland in 1680', *Scots Magazine*, New Series 46 (1947).
26. Royal Commission on Ancient and Historical Monuments in Scotland. 10th Report, Midlothian and West Lothian, reproduced as plate 92.
27. British Museum Satires Catalogue No.747.
28. National Library of Scotland, Adv MS 31.4.22.
29. National Galleries of Scotland, D.3317.
30. British Museum Drawings Catalogue. Anon. Architectural Draughtsman No. 1 (1880–6–12–340).
31. Slezer's 'Particular accompt of Debursements', 1696. Laing IV.
32. Slezer's petition of 22 September 1696. Laing V.

Appendix I The Editions of the *Theatrum Scotiae*.

1693

The first edition had 65 pages of text in addition to the 57 plates of prospects and 32 armorials of the nobility and the Arms of Scotland which adorn the title page. Slezer claims to have printed 150 copies, with 25 copies on 'larger and finer paper'. These are distinguishable from the general run of copies by the watermarks on the paper of the prospects, which have the letters 'TI' in the centre of the sheet.

1718a, 1718b

There were two issues of the *Theatrum Scotiae* in 1718, but the only substantial difference between the two was the number of pages of text. 1718a has 12 pages of text, and 1718b has 43 pages.

1719

This 'edition' is extremely rare and there seems to be no set number or order to the prospects which each individual copy contains. The copy at the National Library of Scotland has 10 pages of text and 37 plates. Some of the plates in this copy are impressions of states which predate the 1718 edition and it may simply be that loose impressions were bound in with the others (an added bit of evidence that Smith actually owned the plates); but so few copies have been recorded, and these differ so considerably, that it might be safer not to regard this as an edition at all.

1728/9

J. Groenowegen and N. Prevost brought out their *Supplement to the Nouveau Theatre de la Grande Bretagne* in 1728. This contained about half the Slezer prints. The next year Joseph Smith issued volume IV of *Nouveau Theatre de la Grande Bretagne*, containing most of the other plates. Neither volume has any text other than a list of contents.

1797

The 1797 issue of the plates is called: *Views of the Principal Towns, Castles, Abbeys &c in Scotland*. There is no text and there are 60 of the plates with the addition of 4 plates by other artists, and a map.

1814

Dr Jamieson issued the last impressions from Slezer's plates in a limited edition of 100. He had the plates of 'Bogengieght', Dryburgh Town, Bothwell Castle, and The Southside of Edinburgh, re-engraved. These plates were printed on different (Whatman) paper with watermarks dated 1810 and 1811, possibly in an attempt not to deceive.

Appendix II
The Plates of the *Theatrum Scotiae*

SL	Prospect	1693	1718	1719	1729/8	1797	Page
1	Edinburgh Castle	1					17
2	Edinburgh	2	2				18–9
3	Dumbarton	3	3	–	56	C.8	20
4	Dumbarton	4	4	–	57	C.7	21
5	Dumbarton	5	5	5	5	√	21
6	Stirling	6	–	47	67	4	22–3
7	Stirling Castle	7	–	48	68	C.2	24
8	Alloa	8	8	8	8	B.9	26
9	Linlithgow	9	9	–	58	16	26
10	Linlithgow Palace	10	10	–	–	C.3	27
11	Falkland	11	11	–	59	15	28
12	Falkland Palace	12	12	12	60	√	29
13	St Andrews	13	–	49	69	9	30
14	St Andrews Cathedral	14	14	–	61	D.1	6, 8, 31
15	St Andrews Castle	15	15	15	15	D.2	31
16	Glasgow Cathedral	17	–	45	65	3	32–3
17	Glasgow	17	–	17	66	2	34
18	Glasgow College	18	18	–	–	–	35
19	New Aberdeen	19	19	–	65	B.2	36
20	Old Aberdeen	20	20	20	20	B.3	37
21	Haddington	21	21	–	–	6	38
22	Lothian	22	22	–	63	B.7	39
23	Montrose	23	–	50	70	B.6	40
24	Dunkeld	24	24	24	64	1	41
25	Dunkeld Cathedral	25	25	–	–	–	41
26	Dunblane	26	26	–	65	8	42
27	Dunblane Cathedral	27	27	–	–	D.3	43
28	Hamilton	28	28	–	67	7	44–5
29	Ayr	29	29	29	68	B.1	46
30	Ayr	30	30	–	69	12	47
31	Dunottar Castle	31	31	–	–	√	48
32	Dryburgh	32	32	–	–	–	50
33	Dryburgh Abbey	33	33	–	70	D.8	51
34	Inverness	34	34	–	–	B.4	52
35	Scone	35	35	35	35	√	52
36	Elgin	36	36	–	71	B.11	53
37	Elgin Cathedral	37	37	–	72	D.4	53
38	Dundee	38	38	38	38	√	54
39	Dundee	39	39	–	–	B.12	55
40	Arbroath	40	40	40	40	B.10	56
41	Arbroath Abbey	41	41	41	73	D.5	57
42	Crossraguel	42	42	42	74	D.6	58
43	(Fortrose)	43	√	51	71	10	58
44	Perth	44	44	–	–	5	59

45	Dunfermline	45	45	–	75	14	60
46	Dunfermline	46	46	–	76	13	61
47	Culross	47	47	–	77	11	62
48	Culross Abbey	48	48	–	–	D.7	63
49	Kelso	49	49	49	49	B.8	64–5
50	Kelso Abbey	50	50	50	78	D.9	66
51	Bothwell Castle	51	51	–	–	–	67
52	Melrose Abbey	52	52	–	79	D.10	7, 68
53	Brechin	53	53	–	80	B.5	68
54	Roslin Chapel	54	54	54	81	D.11	69
55	Paisley	57	57	–	–	√	70
56	The Bass Rock	56	√	54	74	C.4	71
57	The Bass Rock	57	√	53	73	C.5	71
58	Edinburgh (double)	–	?	–	–	–	80–1
58a	Edinburgh (single)	–	–	√?	–	–	
59	Edinburgh Castle	–	?	44	36	C.1	20
60	Stirling Castle	–	√	√	82	17	25
61	Lauder Castle	–	√	√	83	26	82
62	Thirlestane	–	–	58	64	14	83
63	Thirlestane	–	–	59	61	–	82
64	Dalkeith ('Glamms')	–	–	60	77	√	85
65	Gordon ('Inverero')	–	–	61	78	D.12	86
66	Herriot's ('Boghengieght')	–	–	56	√	–	84
67	Hatton ('Argile House')	–	–	57	√	16	84
68	Wemyss ('Donotter')	–	–	55	√	C.6	85
69	Culross House	–	–	52	√	√	63
70	Rothiemay map	–	–	√	58,57	–	
71	Edinburgh (Q. Anne)	–	–	–	55,56	–	
72	'Estampe Emblematique'	–	–	–	√	–	88
73	Glamis	–	–	–	–	–	87

√ = plate included in this edition but un-numbered.

? = an impression of this plate has been recorded in a copy of the 1719 edition other than the copy in the National Library of Scotland.

Index

HMSO publications are available from:

HMSO Bookshops
71 Lothian Road, Edinburgh, EH3 9AZ
031-228 4181 Fax 031-229 2734
49 High Holborn, London, WC1V 6HB
071-873 0011 Fax 071-873 8200 (counter service only)
258 Broad Street, Birmingham, B1 2HE
021-643 3740 Fax 021-643 6510
33 Wine Street, Bristol, BS1 2BQ
0272 264306 Fax 0272 294515
9-21 Princess Street, Manchester, M60 8AS
061-834 7201 Fax 061-833 0634
16 Arthur Street, Belfast, BT1 4GD
0232 238451 Fax 0232 235401

HMSO Publications Centre
(Mail, fax and telephone orders only)
PO Box 276, London, SW8 5DT
Telephone orders 071-873 9090
General enquiries 071-873 0011
(queuing system in operation for both numbers)
Fax orders 071-873 8200

HMSO's Accredited Agents
(see Yellow Pages)
and through good booksellers